OUTLAWS I HAVE KNOWN

OUTLAWS I HAVE KNOWN

AND OTHER REMINISCENCES OF AN INDIAN JUDGE

SIR THEODORE PIGGOTT

GYAN

Published by

Gyan Publishing House
5, Ansari Road
Daryaganj, New Delhi-110002
Phone: 011-47034999, 9811692060
E-mail: books@gyanbooks.com

Distribution Network
gyanbooks.com
India, USA, Canada, UK, Australia

ISBN: 978-93-7097-431-9 (PB)

First Published, 1930

2nd Impression 2025

Printed at: Gyan Press, Delhi.

OUTLAWS I HAVE KNOWN
Arthur SIR THEODORE PIGGOTT

Outlaws I Have Known

And Other Reminiscences of an Indian Judge

BY

SIR THEODORE PIGGOTT

LATE OF THE INDIAN CIVIL SERVICE AND
ONE TIME PUISNE JUDGE OF THE
HIGH COURT OF ALLAHABAD

William Blackwood & Sons Ltd.
Edinburgh and London
1930

CONTENTS.

PART I.

THE BUDAUN DACOITS.

		PAGE
CHAPTER I.	THE PAX BRITANNICA	3
CHAPTER II.	DACOITY IN LAW AND IN FACT	11
CHAPTER III.	ETAH AND BUDAUN	25
CHAPTER IV.	THREE BROTHERS	31
CHAPTER V.	THE PURSUIT	41
CHAPTER VI.	THE ARM OF THE LAW	53
CHAPTER VII.	A TAIL-PIECE	66

PART II.

LEAVES FROM MY CASE-BOOK.

I. ONE FROM JUDGE JEFFREYS' BOOK 77

II. A CLASH OF SUPERSTITIONS 101

III. A MOHARRAM RIOT:

- CHAPTER I. SUNNIS AND SHIAS 122
- CHAPTER II. MOHARRAM IN LUCKNOW . . . 140
- CHAPTER III. MOHARRAM IN AMROHA . . . 166

IV. TWO CHEVALIERS D'INDUSTRIE 192

V. TWO FAILURES OF JUSTICE 221

VI. CHAURI CHAURA:

- CHAPTER I. THE STORY OF THE RIOT . . . 247
- CHAPTER II. THE STORY OF THE TRIAL . . . 279

VII. MISUNDERSTANDINGS 300

PART I.

THE BUDAUN DACOITS

CHAPTER I.

THE PAX BRITANNICA.

THE time will come, I suppose, when the impartial historian will settle down to the task of balancing India's account with England. He will have some complicated matters to go into before answering the question whether any debt of gratitude is due from the former to the latter, from the ward to the self-appointed guardian. The account is still running, and much will depend on whether it can be satisfactorily wound up and the ward be put in effective possession of his own estate without ruinous loss to both parties.

When I entered upon my Indian service a little over forty years ago, it would not have occurred to me to feel any doubts on the subject. I knew that I was to play my small part in an entirely beneficent and civilising mission. It so happened that my first glimpses of the work Englishmen were doing in India were obtained under the influence of that great educationalist, Dr Miller of the Madras Christian College. I still remember the frank delight with which he spoke of the fact that he had come upon two of his pupils engaged in settling a difference of opinion with their fists, quite like Tom Brown and Slogger Williams at Rugby School. There seems to me now something pathetic in this unquestioning belief that the salvation of young India would be found in the steady assimilation of English ideals, if not in the conscious imitation of English ways. I do know, however, that at the Madras Christian College and at the Maharaja of Mysore's College at Bangalore, I saw English education being imparted in an atmosphere in which the relations between the pupils and their foreign tutors retained more than a little of the Hindu tradition of the *chela* and his *guru*, the admiring disciple and the master who was to initiate him in all worthy knowledge. You will not find much of that spirit nowadays amongst the aggressive young Nationalists who throng our Indian universities.

It was some twelve years later, during my first home furlough, that I was brought into contact with an Englishman who had not long retired after a lifetime spent in the service of India. He had been Lieutenant-Governor of a great province, and had brought away with him emphatic proof that his work had won the approval of the greatest Viceroy of my time. His success had been based upon an intimate knowledge of the people in his charge, acquired in the finest of all schools, that of Land Revenue Settlement work, and upon a sympathetic understanding of their character and ideals. We talked much about India; but one remark of his impressed itself on my mind all the more because it was made in connection with a wholly different topic, that of the war in South Africa. "It is not a good thing," he said, "for one nation to charge herself with the destinies of another"; he paused, and added with profound conviction, "it is not good for either of them."

For myself I manage to retain the hope that this will not be the ultimate verdict of history on England's connection with India. I find comfort whenever I cast my mind back over the history of that connection and realise how inevitably, at one stage after another, the charge of India's destinies was thrust upon us by the pressure of events. Once let it be conceded that we were entitled to form settlements in India for purposes of trade, and everything else seems to follow of itself. The distracted state of the country compelled us to enlist armed forces for the protection of our settlements, while the active hostility of the French made it a matter of sheer self-preservation to join in the perilous game of taking sides in the dynastic quarrels and internecine struggles of the Indian States.

To my mind the turning-point came in 1817, when the Marquess of Hastings extorted the reluctant consent of his masters in England to the operations which crushed the Pindaris. We had broken up the Mahratta Confederacy because the Mahrattas would raid outside their own territories, and because we were at war with France and French adventurers were drilling the Mahratta armies; but the victories of Sir Arthur Wellesley and Lord Lake had left chaos outside the East India Company's borders. There were twenty to thirty thousand wild horsemen in scattered bands under various chiefs, ranging the country far and wide in search of plunder: our own territories offered the richest booty, and there was no power outside our borders capable of dealing with the nuisance. When Amir Khan accepted the terms which have made his descendants the Nawabs of Tonk, and Chitu, refusing all terms, died in the tiger's den, we stood committed to the position that we were responsible for peace and order from the Himalayas to Cape Comorin.

We are apt to look upon the establishment and maintenance of the Pax Britannica as our crowning achievement, and one as to the beneficence of which there can be no two opinions. It comes as something of a shock to us when we find the ardent Nationalist of to-day maintaining that there is another side to the shield. He contends that this imposition of peace and order from the outside has 'emasculated' the country; that we have accentuated the process by an Arms Act which leaves the bulk of the population defenceless, and by confining recruitment for the army within the narrow limits of what we are pleased to regard as the 'martial classes.' Speak to him of the anarchy from which we rescued India, or the peril of its return, and you will find that he has been following events farther East with quite other eyes than yours. He looks to see the

Chinese fighting their way, through untold miseries, to the establishment of a settled government on national lines, and believes that it would have been well for his own country in the long-run if she could have been left to do the same.

For good or evil, however, the past history of India is what it is, and the future history of China impossible to forecast. I am not dealing with these things, but with India as I saw it during my thirty-seven years of service. From time to time I have been impelled to ask myself whether Indians generally are really grateful to us for our crowning achievement, whether, in fact, the Pax Britannica is a popular institution. No doubt, to us English security of person and property, the absolute equality of all men beneath the law, have come to be like the air we breathe; we are only conscious of it when it is disturbed, stinted, or polluted. Indians have not our history behind them. I have often felt that numbers of them would gladly exchange the boasted impartiality of our rule for a Government less rigid in its ways, a little readier to make allowances, as for instance, for the feelings of a gentleman and the occasional necessities of his position, or for the claims of a man whose family has done the state good service in the past. "I cannot help thinking," said an Indian gentleman to me not long ago, "that things would be better if the Government of India were a little more concerned with consulting the wishes and taking the advice of its friends, rather than with seeing how far it can possibly go in the way of conciliating its enemies." So as regards this matter of peace and security, I wonder how many Indians there are who feel, subconsciously, that life under the English Raj is a dull affair, devoid of colour or excitement, that its opportunities for advancement are poor at best and limited in effect to those with the opportunity and capacity for assimilating an English education.

Does anyone nowadays read Sir Alfred Lyall's 'Verses Written in India'? He was a man of wide and varied culture, and his verse, like Macaulay's, was a by-product of an active and well-stored mind, but he had genuine gifts of insight and imagination. When, for instance, he desired to criticise the educational policy of the Government of India, he found that he could most effectively do so by placing himself, under his pen-name of Vamadeo Sastri, in the attitude of a Hindu sage of the old school. The best of his verses are dramatic monologues. His "Theology in Extremis" anticipates by many years Conan Doyle's picture of the convinced agnostic driven to choose between instant death and the repetition of a formula, to him perfectly meaningless, professing his conversion to the faith of Islam. In "The Amir's Soliloquy" he has expressed in lines, some of which come home to one curiously in the light of recent events, the sombre and powerful personality of the great Amir Abdurrahman. It is, however, the first poem in the little volume which I would especially commend to the attention of any young man on the threshold of an Indian career—"The Old Pindaree," a soliloquy supposed to be spoken in 1866 by a man of "seventy years well told," pondering over his past life and his present circumstances. The old freebooter, settling down uneasily to the life of a landed proprietor in a changed world, may not be a representative figure in the India of to-day; but his meditations express feelings which no conceivable Government of India can afford to ignore. The stubborn fanaticism of Islam, the offence unwittingly given by some English officials, whether of the energetic and hectoring or of the suavely patronising type; the grim contempt of the illiterate gentleman for a society which offers no scope or outlet for the qualities of courage and leadership which he knows himself to possess; the loathing of the agriculturist for the money-lender and for the cruel jugglery which keeps a debt alive and growing after the principal has been discharged twice over,—all these things are very much alive in that wide India which lies beyond the limits of our semi-Anglicised towns. The glamour of the past is expressed in lines which are worth quoting:—

"It's many a year gone by now; and yet I often dream
Of a long dark march to the Jumna, of splashing across the stream,
Of the waning moon on the water, and the spears in the dim star-light,
As I rode in front of my mother, and wondered at all the sight.

Then, the streak of the pearly dawn—the flash of a sentinel's gun,
The gallop and glint of horsemen who wheeled in the level sun,
The shots in the clear still morning, the white smoke's eddying wreath—
Is this the same land that I live in, the dull dank air that I breathe ? "

One is impelled to wonder how much of Indian unrest at the present day is fundamentally a protest against boredom, the drabness of existence, the absence of excitement and of opportunity. The intelligentsia is finding a growing outlet for its energies in the field of politics ; but here again the violently anti-British attitude, the perilous game of seeing how far you can go before provoking the interference of the law, offers prospects of adventure not to be found in any sober working for constitutional reform.

Away in rural India, in large areas where no word of English is ever spoken, where newspapers do not circulate and books are scarcely to be found, where indeed a surprising percentage of the male population cannot sign their names, those responsible for the administration are constantly brought up against the phenomenon which we call 'dacoity.' The dacoit is not always, I should be prepared to say not usually, a professional criminal as we understand that expression in England. From one point of view he may be said to voice the protest of rural India against the Pax Britannica.

CHAPTER II.

DACOITY IN LAW AND IN FACT.

IT is stated in Lord Macaulay's biography that during his five years in India he rendered that country two great services, the more admirable because the work done in connection with each of them was 'voluntary and unpaid.' As Chairman of the Board of Education, he laid down the broad lines on which Englishmen were to undertake the task of conferring upon India the blessings of Western education. As President of the Commission appointed for the purpose, he was mainly responsible for the first draft of the Indian Penal Code. Now Macaulay was a great writer, a man of wide reading and inspired with a passionate love of what was best in literature. His warmest admirer would not have thought of describing him as a great lawyer. Yet his success in the second of his two undertakings was as conspicuous as his failure in the first.

I should be straying too far from my subject if I embarked upon a criticism of the educational system for which Macaulay was primarily responsible. Of the radical defect in his policy he was not even remotely conscious. His energies concentrated upon the controversy, important enough in its way, but quite subsidiary, whether higher education should be directed towards Western Literature or the older Oriental Classics; he took it for granted that the creation of an educated class at the top of the social scale would be followed automatically by the filtering of knowledge downward through the masses. This expectation has been brought to the test of practical experience, and has disastrously failed. The country needed two generations of widespread and intensive training in primary and secondary schools before it was ripe for the University system Macaulay imposed on it in the late 'thirties. It may be that as an old man I dream dreams, but I do wonder what India would be like to-day if its Government had determined, ninety years ago, to devote its available resources in men and money first of all to the creation of a network of primary schools where lads might learn to read and write their own vernaculars in the Roman character, with secondary schools provided, as the demand for them arose, to carry instruction further, through the same media. English Education and Western Science would have followed in due course, mainly at the expense of those who wanted them and in the form best suited to their needs.

My digression has carried me too far already and I must get back to the Indian Penal Code. Here we have another story altogether, that of a great piece of work which has stood the test of time. It seems indeed to have had a dazzling effect on the eyes of those for whose benefit it was first produced. Macaulay's successors in office spent twenty years making notes upon it and accustoming their minds to its daring originality; it needed the great upheaval of the Mutiny to force the Code on to the statute-book. Nevertheless it arrived there with surprisingly little modification; the one chapter which was substantially re-written, that on Homicide, remains on the whole the least satisfactory portion of the Code. One cannot quote a greater authority on the codification of law than that of Sir James Fitzjames Stephen. His verdict on the Indian Penal Code is that "it reproduces in a concise and even beautiful form the spirit of the Law of England in a compass which, by comparison with the original, may be regarded as almost absurdly small."

In the matter of what they call 'dacoity,' however, the framers of the Indian Penal Code were dealing with a form of crime scarcely known in England, but which they rightly held to demand very special treatment. It is interesting to see how they set about it. To arrive at their definition the student must work back to the sections which put into legal terms the concepts of 'theft' and of 'extortion.' He will then come to section 390, which deals with 'robbery'; I think it worth quoting.

"In all robbery there is either theft or extortion. Theft is 'robbery,' if in order to the committing of the theft, or in committing the theft, or in carrying away or attempting to carry away property obtained by the theft, the offender, for that end, voluntarily causes or attempts to cause to any person death, or hurt, or wrongful restraint, or fear of instant death, or of instant hurt, or of instant wrongful restraint.

" Extortion is 'robbery' if the offender, at the time of committing the extortion, is in the presence of the person put in fear, and commits the extortion by putting that person in fear of instant death, of instant hurt, or of instant wrongful restraint to that person, or to some other person, and, by so putting in fear, induces the person so put in fear then and there to deliver up the thing extorted."

I omit a brief explanation intended to clear up all possible doubt as to when the offender may be said to be in the presence of the person put in fear, but pause to warn the reader that the expressions 'hurt' and 'wrongful restraint' are themselves carefully defined in antecedent sections of the Code. We are now ready for section 391—

" When five or more persons conjointly commit or attempt to commit a robbery, or where the whole number of persons conjointly committing or attempting to commit a robbery, and persons present and aiding such commission or attempt, amount to five or more, every person so committing, attempting, or aiding is said to commit 'dacoity.'"

Having thus arrived at a definition of what we might call gang-robbery, the legislature proceeds to deal with it in the sternest fashion. Departing from its almost invariable practice, the Code prescribes a minimum as well as a maximum sentence in certain cases. An important section lays down that if any one of five or more persons, who are conjointly committing dacoity, commits murder in so committing dacoity, every one of those persons shall be liable to the punishment for murder, which in India may be either death or transportation for life. Special sections prescribe punishments for belonging to a gang of persons associated for the purpose of habitually committing dacoity, or for being one of five or more persons assembled for the purpose of committing a single dacoity. Even more remarkable is section 399, which renders liable to imprisonment for a maximum term of ten years "whoever makes any preparation for committing dacoity."

Moralists have often insisted on the gulf which, in matters of crime, separates thought from deed, the intention from the act. Listen a moment to Thomas Carlyle—

> "From the purpose of crime to the act of crime there is an abyss; wonderful to think of. The finger lies on the pistol; but the man is not yet a murderer: nay his whole nature staggering at such consummation, is there not a confused pause rather—one last instant of possibility for him? Not yet a murderer; it is at the mercy of light trifles whether the most fixed idea may not yet become unfixed. One slight twitch of a muscle, the death-flash bursts; and he is it, and will for Eternity be it."

There are only two classes of crime in dealing with which the Indian Penal Code sees fit to ignore this distinction and to make mere 'preparation' a punishable offence. Dacoity is one; the other is what we call in England 'high treason,' and in India 'waging war on the king.'

There are good reasons for this; their consideration I can best introduce by another quotation from Fitzjames Stephen—

> "It must be borne in mind what crime in India is. Here in England, order is so thoroughly well established that the crime of the country is hardly more than an annoyance. In India, if crime is allowed to get to a head it is capable of destroying the peace and prosperity of whole tracts of country. The mass of the people in their common moods are gentle, submissive, and disposed to be innocent; but, for that very reason, bold and successful criminals are dangerous in the extreme. In old days, when they joined in gangs and organised bodies, they soon acquired political importance. Now, in many parts of India, crime is quite as uncommon as in the least criminal parts of England; and the old high-handed systematised crime has almost entirely disappeared. This great revolution (for it is nothing less) in the state of society of a whole continent has been brought about by the regular administration of a rational body of criminal law."

The reference to the 'political importance' of the leaders of gangs of freebooters is probably due to reminiscences of the Pindaris, but the phenomenon of dacoity has its political aspect. After the annexation of Upper Burma we dealt with, under the name of 'dacoity,' a great deal of what might not unfairly have been described as guerilla warfare against foreign invaders.

William the Conqueror, if he had known the word, would probably have described Hereward the Wake as a dacoit leader; and Edward I. obviously regarded William Wallace in much the same light. We English, who have made a hero of Robin Hood, should not find it difficult to understand the attitude of a peasant community towards the daring outlaw, in open rebellion against the powers that be, whose plundering raids are mostly directed against rack-renting landholders, profiteering shopkeepers, or usurers who grind the faces of the poor.

I propose to tell in some detail the story of the most remarkable dacoits with whom I was ever brought into personal contact, but before doing so I want to give English readers a general idea of the methods followed in the carrying out of a typical dacoity. The organisers will probably be two or three men who have worked together before, and are ready for another venture. They are quite possibly small landholders or substantial cultivators, still ostensibly earning an honest livelihood. The 'outlaw' stage, the time when there is a warrant out for his arrest, when he can no longer show himself openly in a place where he is known, or visit his home except by stealth, is reached by the successful dacoit leader in due course, but he may have brought off many a lucrative raid before he is reduced to that extremity. The intended victim is marked down days in advance, after much careful discussion of alternative schemes and probably a reconnoitring

visit or two by trusted agents. The collection of the gang is done carefully and methodically by personal visits on the part of the organisers, or messages sent here and there through trusted subordinates. For an important raid some twenty to thirty men will be required, and a vital question is the provision of arms. Every man will carry at least the quarterstaff of stout bamboo which is the national weapon of the peasantry of Northern India; an old sword or two, and now and then an axe or a spear come in handy, but the great desideratum is firearms. The leaders, if they are worth their salt, know where to lay their hands on some old fowling-piece or a bell-mouthed blunderbuss, carefully hidden away along with a scanty store of ammunition. They are probably in touch with one or more desperate men, already outlaws evading arrest, who can be relied on to bring at least an old pistol along with them to the rendezvous. They know, also, the location of every registered and licensed firearm in the neighbourhood, the owner of which will lend it for a consideration without asking inconvenient questions. One way or another from three to six firearms of sorts can be got together for an important raid. The night must be chosen carefully, with due consideration for the state of the weather and the phases of the moon. The rendezvous where the gang will gather by twos and threes must not be too near the scene of operations, lest alarm be given beforehand. Nor must it be too far off, because the cross-country

march of a body of men is apt to leave traces behind it which can be followed up later on by an intelligent police officer. A similar objection applies to a journey by train, though I have come across dacoits who have known how to make our railway time-tables distinctly useful. The question of commissariat offers no difficulties; any Indian peasant can do a day's work on a handful of parched grain and a few sweetmeats. The use of clarified butter in the preparation of the latter evades all caste difficulties about cooked food, for butter is a product of the sacred cow. The gang will approach their destination soon after dark, and here they will be joined, nine times out of ten, by one or two local men who have been admitted to the plot, often because they are known to be at feud with the intended victim. Every dacoit leader worth his salt recognises the importance of having someone with him who knows the lie of the land, the precise situation and tenancy of neighbouring houses, the twists and turns of village lanes.

The house to be attacked will be closed and bolted for the night, but ways of gaining admission are various. The courtyard wall can usually be scaled by determined men making use of bamboo poles and one another's shoulders, or the local man may lead the way to a little house next door, with no defence but a flimsy hurdle and no resident but a poor widow, from the roof of which three or four men can climb on to the flat roof of the wealthy house which is their goal. Meanwhile, as

likely as not, six or seven bold spirits will march up to the main door, hammering upon it and demanding admission in the name of the law; they are police officers in mufti and must see the owner of the house at once. One way or another the outer door is opened from the inside and the dacoits stream in. Their first step must be to light blazing fires in the courtyard and just outside the main door; there is always a thatched shed somewhere, and kerosene oil to be poured upon the thatch. Light they must have at all costs, not only for their work of plunder inside, but lest resolute villagers crowd in upon them through the darkness and they find themselves involved in a fight at close quarters. For further precaution against this there will be some miscellaneous discharging of firearms, and usually one man with gun or blunderbuss will mount guard outside. If the raiders come from a distance there is little or no attempt at disguise, but the older hands know the advantage of drawing a fold of the turban round under the chin, covering both sides of the face and leaving little visible but the mouth and eyes.

The main quest will be for cash and jewellery. There will be stores of both buried somewhere or other under the mud floor in an inner room; now and then the subsequent trial will reveal grim stories as to the measures adopted to compel the disclosure of these hiding-places. I can myself remember a case in which I sternly enforced the extremest powers of an Indian High Court, en-

hancing the sentence passed by the trial Judge, in order to exact the death penalty from members of a gang some of whom had flung a young child into the blazing fire to compel its parents to say where they had hidden their valuables. Happily such cases of extreme brutality are rare ; a certain stoical resignation to adverse fate is inherent in Indian character, and the victims will usually avoid provoking their assailants. The women of the household huddled together in some inner room will be compelled to deliver up what ornaments they are wearing. Often considerable booty will be collected in the shape of wearing apparel and stores of cloth, while, in the case of a raid upon a money-lender's house, the dacoits will rarely miss the opportunity of acquiring popularity by flinging into their bonfire any bonds or books of account on which they can lay hands. They must get away well before daylight to allow time for a rough division of the booty and an unobtrusive return to their several homes.

I am tempted to insert here, by way of tailpiece to this chapter, a reminiscence which cropped up while I wrote of the dacoit on guard at the house door. To make it intelligible to English readers I must concoct a phrase on the analogy of ' brown-bess,' the name by which the private soldier in old times designated his flint-lock musket. There was an Indian name for an ancient type of firearm which similarly suggested a personal name, but in this case of the male sex: let us call it a ' black-sammy.' A witness at a dacoity

trial singled out one of the accused, Jiwan Singh, whom he happened, by the merest accident, to have met before, and said that he saw him in the light of the bonfire just in front of the house. He was pressed in cross-examination as to his opportunities for accurate observation. "I was watching him for some time," he said; "he was walking up and down *with (a) black-sammy.*" At any rate that was what the witness meant to say, but there was no place in his vocabulary for the indefinite article, and the word he used for the dacoit's weapon was so obsolete that neither the Judge nor any of the counsel engaged in the case had ever heard it before. Consequently the words which I have put in italics appeared in the Judge's English record as: "*accompanied by swarthy Samuel.*" In cross-examination the witness was asked if Samuel was one of the other accused present in court; he was puzzled by the question, but merely replied that he knew none of them by that name and did not identify any except Jiwan Singh and one or two others whom he had picked out in a different connection. The next witness on the point identified Jiwan Singh as having been on guard at the door, and added that he had seen him point his musket down the lane at some villagers who were stealing up through the darkness; here he used the ordinary name for the firearm and it appeared that he had not a word to say about 'Samuel.' Jiwan Singh's counsel was now hot upon the scent of a serious discrepancy in the evidence. The unfortunate

witness was bombarded with questions which left him hopelessly bamboozled; if they meant Samuel of the neighbouring village of Dustypore, he was a dark-complexioned man enough, but he had not seen him amongst the dacoits nor had he noticed that any other dacoit was patrolling the front of the house along with Jiwan Singh. As the trial progressed confusion grew worse confounded. It is quite inevitable that information of what is going on in the court should filter through to the witnesses who are waiting outside. In this case the information must have taken the form that the Judge had private reasons for knowing that Samuel of Dustypore had taken part in the dacoity, and moreover, was inclined to be testy with witnesses who had seen nothing of Samuel. What were the bewildered peasants to do? If the Judge said Samuel had been concerned in the business, he was most probably right. Anyhow, Samuel was not on his trial, there was plenty of time to make inquiries about him when they got home. The immediate question was whether these brutes who had plundered their village and injured some of their neighbours were to escape punishment, merely because no one had hitherto thought of Samuel's being concerned in the affair. Before the trial came to an end two or three witnesses were quite sure they had seen Samuel amongst the dacoits, and furnished the Judge with wildly discrepant accounts of Samuel's doings. The unhappy police officer responsible for the investigation could only say that he had not arrested

Samuel of Dustypore because he had not heard a syllable against the man in the course of his inquiry.

The Judge was frankly puzzled, but did not allow this side-issue to confuse his view of the entire case. He found Jiwan Singh and some others guilty and sentenced them accordingly. As to Samuel of Dustypore, he thought there should be further inquiry; it looked as if the man had contrived to bring influence to bear on the witnesses to keep his name out of it.

An appeal lies to the High Court, on the facts as well as the law, in all cases tried by a Sessions Judge without the aid of a jury. The case came before a bench of two Judges, one of whom could look back on many years of service, some of them spent in the district from which the case came. By this time the learned counsel representing Jiwan Singh had worked out a really plausible theory. The villain of the piece was Samuel of Dustypore, a dangerous criminal with a heart as black as his complexion. He had overawed the witnesses, had probably bribed the police, had arranged it that the witnesses were to ascribe to the unfortunate Jiwan Singh everything that they had actually seen done by this consummate villain. It was a great effort, which only broke down on the long experience and tenacious memory of the senior Judge. The latter turned to the verbatim transcript of the depositions as recorded in the vernacular simultaneously with the Judge's English notes, and he knew what a 'black-sammy' was when he came to it. Jiwan Singh served his time.

CHAPTER III.

ETAH AND BUDAUN.

THE districts of Etah and Budaun, in the province of Agra, face one another across the Ganges, the former on the right bank and the latter on the left, at a point where the great river, having completed its southward course, is entering upon that eastward trend which carries it, past Cawnpore, Allahabad, and Benares, to the far distant sea. Budaun is the more important historically; during the thirteenth century its governors furnished two rulers to the imperial throne at Delhi, before it fell under the power of the Rohillas, was taken from them by the Nawab of Oudh and by him ceded to the British in 1801. Etah was a prosperous land, rich in temples and monasteries when it was visited by the Chinese Buddhist pilgrim, Hsuan Tsang, in the seventh century of our era. It fell upon troublous times later on, was occupied by Rajput immigrants, conquered by Moslem invaders under Mahmud of Ghazni, and passed into British hands, along with the territory on the opposite side of the Ganges, by cession from the Nawab of Oudh.

I arrived in Budaun in the early spring of 1893 to take over the subordinate position of Joint-Magistrate and Assistant Collector. That summer the charge of the district was held, as a temporary measure, by Mr J. S. (now Lord) Meston, who laid the foundations of his brilliant career by his work on the revision of the Land Revenue Settlement. At the commencement of the cold weather he was relieved of the charge of the district by the arrival of a senior officer from leave, the distinguished scholar and archæologist, Mr Vincent Smith. I retain memories of my three years' service in Budaun which I must not be tempted into entering upon here. I do sometimes wonder whether that doughty upholder of the Caliphate and intransigent Nationalist, Maulana Shaukat Ali, ever calls to mind the brilliant innings he played on the Budaun parade ground in order to win for the Aligarh College what was destined to be the first of a number of victories over scratch Elevens, laboriously collected by me in the course of the next ten years or so. Shaukat Ali was a great leader on the cricket field.

The Budaun district has been opened up since my time by railway extensions which have linked up the narrow-gauge lines on the two sides of the Ganges. In 1893 the nearest railway station was nineteen miles from headquarters ; there can have been few better districts in India for duck and snipe, while black-buck were plentiful. A population of about a million souls in an area of just under two thousand square miles left room for large tracts of waste land, swamps, and scrub-jungle and sandy dunes.

It will save me a digression later if I set down a few words here about a feature of my work in Budaun which I found most enjoyable, my superintendence of the annual bathing festival known as the Kakora Mela. The day of the November full moon is a sacred day of the Hindus, one on which particular merit attaches to the ceremonial bath taken in the Ganges or any of its tributaries, or for the matter of that in running water anywhere. Apart from the recognised holy places such as Hardwar, Allahabad, and Benares, there are certain localities on the great river where people gather in large numbers for this particular festival. At the commencement of the cold season, when the rains were fairly over and the Ganges could be trusted to have settled down into a definite channel as its flood waters subsided, it was my first duty to send out my tents in the direction of the river-bank and choose a site for the fair. It had to be within the limits of certain lands owned by the Mohammedan landholders of Shekhupur, but might be fixed anywhere within a stretch of five miles or more of river-bank, the great desideratum being a bend of river affording plenty of shallow water with a gentle flow of the current. I still remember the slight incredulity with which, on the first occasion, I found myself riding along desolate sandbanks miles away from anything like a substantial village, while my Indian subordinates and the steward of the local landholders discussed the layout of a camp capable of accommodating two hundred thousand souls. We had to fix the site of a central police station, and of its outposts, of a dispensary, of the tents to be occupied by the officials who were to camp at the fair itself, besides finding a suitable grove not too far distant for the English officials who would come down for the week. A thousand details of sanitation, approach roads, with the bridging of one or more of the shallow backwaters which the retreating floods nearly always left behind them, at varying distances from the main bank, called for attention, let alone the policing of the fair itself and the roads leading to it. Preliminaries settled, I might go about my other work for a month or so, returning some ten days before the full moon to find the place beginning to fill up. Day after day, from all directions, strings of carts laden to their utmost capacity converged upon the spot until a veritable city of shops, booths, tents of every description sprung into being. For the ordinary villager and his family the cart in which they had made the journey was readily convertible into a temporary home.

I wish I could convey to English readers even a pale reflection of the fascination I found in an Indian bathing fair, the riot of colour under the glorious sunshine, the joyous animation of the crowds. My memories turned irresistibly in that direction when I read a certain deplorable book on the sorrows of Indian womankind. I felt that if it were given me to take the authoress of 'Mother

India' to Kakora or Garhmuktesar on the day of a November full moon, I could ask her whether the magnificent specimens of humanity visible all about us did not at least suggest a doubt as to the actual proportion of Indian babies coming into the world under the hideous conditions which she describes as normal, if not universal; also whether the sheer joyousness of the great concourse, and particularly of the female half of it, might not contribute a splash of brightness to the sombre colours of her palette.

I was in charge of the Kakora Mela for three consecutive years. I worked hard over it and enjoyed every hour of it. In the third year I received, at the hands of the Mohant or Abbot of a certain order of Hindu ascetics, what I long regarded as the greatest compliment paid me on my work in India. It was almost thirty years later that my old friend, Sir Charles Ross Alston, bidding me good-bye and God-speed in the name of the Allahabad bar, added something to which I give the first place in my memories in this kind.

When I wrote above that I enjoyed every moment of my work as superintendent of the bathing fair, I was overlooking certain days during my first year in charge which found me cursing my ill-fortune in being tied down to this particular job instead of tasting the sweets of adventure elsewhere. We had just completed our arrangements that year and the first rills of the great concourse were trickling in, when certain rumours began to reach us, reinforced presently by urgent official instructions for the taking of special precautions at the fair itself and along the roads leading to it: Bijai Singh's gang of dacoits had crossed the river from the Etah side and were at large in our district. The Superintendent of Police, Mr C. G. Denne, was absent from our camp at Kakora, scouring the country in pursuit of the raiders. The wildest stories were in circulation as to their exploits, culminating in the circumstantial report of a serious dacoity with murder committed at a village farther north on the other side of Budaun City. Some days later a runner came in from headquarters with news that Mr Denne had had a brush with the gang, had been himself wounded, but believed that he held them hemmed in so that their capture was possible if reinforcements could reach him in time. My orders were to remain at my post, and I watched with sick envy the other two English officials in the camp mounting their ponies for a cross-country ride which they hoped might bring them to the scene of action before it was too late. I was destined to make the acquaintance of the dacoit leaders later on, both in my judicial and in my executive capacity: it is their story which I now propose to tell.

CHAPTER IV.

THREE BROTHERS.

THE three brothers, Pohpi Singh, Dhara Singh, and Bijai Singh, were landholders of a small village in a remote part of the Etah District. They belonged to one of the old Hindu fighting clans, being probably the descendants of immigrants from Rajputana. A hundred years earlier they might well have risen to fame and fortune as guerilla leaders in a troubled land, but their restless and turbulent spirits failed to accommodate themselves to the conditions of their own day, under a government invincibly prejudiced against men who "take the law into their own hands." They were ill neighbours to get on with, not content to regard a grievance against another landholder as a matter to be fought out through the chicanery of the law courts. To them it was a case for reprisals in the way of looting of cattle and crops or the burning of byres. This kind of thing means, sooner or later, friction with the local police; it is very apt also to lead to an increasing association with professional criminals and the organising of raids for purposes of gain as well as of revenge. The officer in charge of an outlying police station is often none too scrupulous in his methods of dealing with men to whose disadvantage he suspects a great deal more than he can support by genuine evidence. Pohpi Singh himself, a shrewd and level-headed man of fifty or so, acquired considerable dexterity in dealing with the criminal courts. His moment of triumph came when he succeeded in bringing one of his differences with the local police to final adjudication by a learned Judge of the Allahabad High Court, and secured a judgment which was for a time a treasured possession, a sort of charter of freedom for the family: it described the brothers as "respectable landholders engaged in an unequal struggle against the petty tyranny of subordinate police officers."

If Pohpi Singh had been alone he might perhaps have carried on after this within the limits of the law, but his brothers were not made of quite the same stuff. Dhara Singh was to prove himself a born soldier, utterly fearless and capable of inspiring courage in others, as well as of enforcing rough discipline on unpromising material. For the present his overbearing temper and stubborn vindictiveness were the qualities which most influenced the family fortunes in the wrong direction. Bijai Singh was considerably the youngest of the three, and beyond question his brothers were very fond of him. I think it was this affection on their part, along with his good looks and a certain dignity of bearing, which led to his being put forward later on as the titular leader of the gang. On any of their raids on which they found it convenient to impersonate a party of police in mufti it was always Bijai Singh who figured as the 'Darogha Sahib,' the police officer in command. He chafed more than the others over the narrowness of the family means, which as a matter of fact were in a bad way. They had got into the hands of moneylenders, and mortgages were accumulating at compound interest on the family estate.

Thus it was that Pohpi Singh's house became more and more notorious as a rendezvous for bad characters, and the officer in charge of the local police station increasingly certain that dacoit raids upon unpopular moneylenders and the houses of wealthy traders were being organised from that house as a base. He bided his time until he had collected evidence which would stand the test of the most searching judicial examination, but when he arrived with his warrants of arrest he found the birds flown. The brothers had gone into hiding; henceforth their home was a place to which they could return only by stealth and for brief intervals. They gathered unto them other spirits worse than themselves, and it was at the head of a gang of close upon thirty desperate men, the great majority of them outlaws like themselves, that Pohpi Singh crossed the river into the Budaun District.

He must have organised his gang with much forethought. They were better armed than the ordinary run of dacoits. Pohpi Singh himself had somehow acquired an excellent double-barrelled smoothbore, and there were six or eight other firearms distributed amongst his followers, with no lack of ammunition. They had with them a fair number of ponies and were obviously bent on increasing the mobility of the force by acquiring more mounts as occasion offered. Besides the three brothers there were two other men amongst the outlaws who call for individual notice. Komil Singh was the reckless ne'er-do-weel of a respectable family. He had squandered more money than the rest had ever owned between them before bad company drew him on to active participation in crime, and a warrant of arrest drove him into hiding. The second man to whom I have referred was Bhawan, a *brahman* by caste and a wrestler by profession, a beetle-browed ruffian with the strength, the savagery, and the intelligence of a gorilla.

One is inclined to wonder whether men of this sort, virtually at war with the Government of India, could have any plans for the future, any outlook upon life beyond that of evading as long as possible the inevitable clash against superior forces, and in the meantime enjoying life after their own fashion. For I take it to be beyond doubt that the life of a professional outlaw has a definite fascination for certain spirits. 'Once a dacoit always a dacoit' was a saying of Sir H. Sleeman's, who knew this side of Indian life as few, if any, Englishmen have done since his time. In this particular case I formed so high an opinion of Pohpi Singh's intelligence, and found such traces of method in his proceedings, that I cannot believe him to have been wholly desperate or without some considered scheme for the future. Up to a certain point he led his men across the Budaun District in a generally northward direction, and he was unquestionably trying to convert his following into an efficiently mounted force. Police officers engaged in the pursuit thought at one time that he was making for the territories of the Nawab of Rampur, that fragment of the old Rohilla monarchy which retains a qualified independence; but another rumour credited him with the bolder design of working his way across the wild territory along the foot of the Himalayas into the kingdom of Nepal. It is conceivable that such a body of men, if they could make their way beyond the territories administered by the British Government, with cash and jewellery in their hands sufficient to constitute an adequate bribe for some local official, might find an asylum, and even lands to cultivate, or other profitable employment.

In their progress across the district the gang followed a certain routine. They marched at night, camping for the day either on waste lands or at some suitable spot within the boundaries of a cultivated village. A plot of land lying fallow in the midst of tall crops of sugar-cane or millet makes an admirable camping ground. Subsequent inquiries put it beyond doubt that they had received shelter and supplies of food from landholders in more than one village; probably Pohpi Singh knew beforehand where to find villages owned or controlled by sympathetic caste-fellows, or by men who had previously dabbled in the perilous game of 'harbouring dacoits' in return for a share of the booty. Now and again it happened that a stray wayfarer stumbled on the dacoit encampment; if so, he was detained until moonrise and sent about his business half an hour before the gang started on their next march. Any news of their whereabouts which reached Mr Denne from this source was never less than a couple of days old. Once and again, the plunder of a moneylender's house in one place and that of an unpopular landholder in another, served to keep the gang in funds. Their most daring exploit was the lifting of a valuable saddle-horse belonging to the sub-inspector in charge of Ujhani Police Station, which that officer had left tethered outside his private quarters.

One other raid they attempted in quest of a similar addition to their means of transport which turned out disastrously for themselves. At the subsequent trial we called it 'the raid on the *Ahar* village.' Now, the *Ahars* of Budaun are a sub-caste with definite characteristics of their own. Orthodox Hinduism regards them as nothing higher than a subdivision of the caste of *Ahirs*, or herdsmen, inclined to give themselves airs and to call attention to the fact by a slight variation in the spelling of the clan name. They themselves repudiate all connection with the *Ahirs* and claim to be a fragment of an old Kshattriya clan. They are a sturdy and independent folk; in the days of the Mutiny they took a definite line of their own. They rallied round the *Tahsildar*, the petty Magistrate and Revenue Officer at Gunnaur, in the north-west corner of the district, and kept him in office for weeks after the rest of the district was under the control of the rebels. In fact, the Mohammedan and Hindu factions at Budaun City had to suspend the internecine struggle they had been waging ever since the flight of the English officials, and send a joint force against Gunnaur, including some regular troops. Even then the sturdy *Ahars* stood up to them and were only beaten after a hard fight.

It was a little village owned by these *Ahars* which attracted the notice of Pohpi Singh and his men, by reason of the fact that the landholders were known to possess an exceptionally valuable mare. When they marched into the place the villagers rallied to the rescue. With no better weapons than their bamboo staffs they stood up to the marauders, pelted them with brickbats from house roofs, held their ground after three of their number had been shot down, and maintained a struggle at close quarters while the owners of the mare dug through the mud wall at the back of the stable and got the animal away to a place of safety. I am glad to be able to add that none of the three *Ahars* was fatally injured, that we gave handsome rewards, especially to one man who was crippled for life, and that identification evidence from this village weighed heavily against certain of the dacoits at their trial.

In spite of this failure, Pohpi Singh and Dhara Singh had by this time succeeded in organising a force capable of considerable mobility. They were close on the northern border of the Budaun District, within easy reach of the Rampur State, and not many marches away from the wild Terai country along the Himalayan foothills. That they turned back at this point and became involved in an adventure fraught with fatal consequences was due to two of their followers, those whom I have already singled out for separate mention.

Komil Singh, in his days of affluence, had entertained as his mistress a dancing-girl of the name of Shahzadi. She appeared in my court later, a brazen-faced hussy, handsome in her way and reputed to be a more than competent musician. When Komil Singh disappeared from reputable society she passed under the protection of a caste-fellow of his, by name Ghanshiam Singh, a landholder of village Laindheri, some thirteen miles north of Budaun city. It was Komil Singh who now suggested that Ghanshiam Singh's house would be worth plundering; for himself he desired revenge on the man who had supplanted him, and to recover possession of his light-of-love. I have always suspected that Pohpi Singh was none too anxious to encumber his party with a woman, one moreover whose presence might breed dissensions; it was also foreign to his character and contrary to his past record to lead his men on an expedition having stark murder for one of its predetermined objectives. In all probability it was due to some precaution on his part that warning reached Ghanshiam Singh in time, though only just in time. On a mild November evening that worthy was entertaining friends on the masonry platform outside his house, the fair Shahzadi beguiling the company with selections from her repertoire to her own accompaniment on the zither. There came down the village street an elderly man leaning on his long bamboo staff. He was a landholder from a neighbouring village, Sahbi Singh by name, a caste-fellow of Ghanshiam Singh's and a previous acquaintance, though there was no particular intimacy between them.

After the usual salutations the old man spoke. "My reason for coming round this evening was to bring you a piece of news. I happen to know that Bijai Singh's dacoits intend to pay you a visit in a few hours' time. They are after your fair charmer here, and it will go hard with you, brother Ghanshiam, if they find you at home." The little party broke up in such haste that the zither was left behind, to be carried off by the dacoits—one wonders if Komil Singh attached a sentimental value to its possession—and to prove an interesting item of circumstantial evidence against them. At any rate, Ghanshiam Singh and his mistress got into safe hiding, and to this extent the warning proved effectual.

Unhappily, it occurred to his kindly neighbour, almost at the last moment, to carry his good offices a step further. " I'll wait here," he said as the others were hastening off ; " when I tell them that you have got away and taken the lady with you, possibly they may not plunder your house." They left him pipe and tobacco and he sat composedly down on the raised platform. At dusk the outlaws streamed into the village with no attempt at secrecy or disguise, but on the contrary discharging their firearms at random to overawe the villagers. They came to a halt in the narrow lane ; and " Ho ! Ghanshiam Singh ! " cried a voice. Sahbi Singh stood up raising one arm ; " Listen to me, you men," he began. The wrestler, Bhawan, came thrusting to the front, a gross insult on his lips. " Get out of the way, you sweeper," he called. Sahbi Singh swung up his quarterstaff ; " I am no sweeper," he said, " but a *thakur*, and I'll break the head of the next man who uses that name to me." And thereupon Bhawan shot him dead, shot him down like a dog on the doorstep of the house he had undertaken to defend. The die was cast now, the outlaws came swarming in over the corpse. They plundered that house and two others before marching off, laden with booty and intoxicated with the sense of lawless power.

CHAPTER V.

THE PURSUIT.

To Pohpi Singh and his brothers the Laindheri dacoity proved fatal in more ways than one. Men who embark upon the commission of a crime which can only be carried through by the aid of ruffians more savage and reckless than themselves incur a grave responsibility for crimes which their accomplices may find occasion to commit in prosecution of the common aim. This principle is recognised by the Indian Penal Code, and those charged with the administration of the law in India are apt to be stern in its enforcement as against dacoits who go about their business with firearms in their hands. Moreover, the murder of Sahbi Singh had been a singularly brutal act. Henceforth the shadow of the gallows walked before the footsteps of the gang.

In the second place, they had run a grave risk in venturing to raid a village barely more than thirteen miles from Budaun city, and it so happened that Mr Denne had just returned to headquarters that evening. He had had a poor time of it during the previous week. It was a slur on his administration that this notorious gang of outlaws should be marching at large about his district, but his difficulties were great. He had no mounted men at his disposal, the handful of armed police available for the pursuit were ill-trained for long-distance marching; his news of the dacoits was rarely less than forty-eight hours old, and they had been keeping steadily on the move. He was a weary and disheartened man when he reached Budaun. He had outmarched his tents and his commissariat and found accommodation for the night in a spare tent pitched in the compound of the Collector's house. Alongside of him was camped the Civil Surgeon, who happened to have newly reached Budaun upon transfer and had found that his bungalow needed repairs.

He, by the way, was L. G. Fischer, the old Edinburgh University and Scottish international half-back. It remains one of the minor coincidences of my life that I should have watched Fischer helping his University to inflict upon mine the first defeat which the magnificent Oxford fifteens of those days had suffered for two seasons, only to make his acquaintance nine years later as a member of the small European community of Budaun, and the husband of an old friend of my wife's girlhood. Vincent Smith, Fischer, and Denne dined together that night, discussed possible plans of action in a somewhat pessimistic mood, and retired to rest all the earlier because Fischer was badly wanted to supervise the medical arrangements at Kakora, and was due to start early the following morning. At about two o'clock at night a runner came in from Laindheri with the news.

Denne was afoot at once; here was news of his quarry only a few hours old. A messenger brought up six or eight men from the armed police lines; he slung his gun across his shoulders, strapped a few provisions on to his saddle and prepared to start. He had just mounted when Fischer came running up. The significance of the hasty dialogue which ensued was only realised later.

"Would you like my rifle?" asked Fischer.

"No," was the reply, "the shot-gun is lighter to carry, and if there is any shooting to be done it will be at close quarters."

"What cartridges have you got?"

"I haven't looked to see, but I've got this belt full." Fischer ran into his tent and came back with two handfuls of number threes. "Take these, anyhow"; Denne stuffed them into his pockets and rode off. It was six days later when he discovered that the rest of his ammunition consisted of snipe-shot.

The preceding five days had been a dreary business. The dacoits had left Laindheri in a direction which accorded with the preconceived idea that they were making for the Rampur border, and the pursuit started in that direction. Then news came in which indicated that the gang had doubled back and were working southwards and eastwards. Pohpi Singh probably realised that, after the Laindheri murder, he and his men had become too important criminals to hope for shelter or connivance from any official of the Rampur State. He headed for the sparsely settled tract lying about the confluence of the Ganges with its tributary the Ramgunga, a point from which he could, if hard pressed, recross the main river into his own district of Etah. On this new line the pursuit continued, tentatively, with casts in this direction and in that upon a scent that steadily grew colder and colder. By the evening of the fifth day Denne marched his weary men into a substantial village far down in the south-eastern corner of his district; he was thoroughly disheartened and his quarry seemed to have definitely eluded him.

The local landholder received the police party with anxious hospitality. No, he had heard nothing of any dacoits in that neighbourhood; he would send out men to make inquiries, especially in the direction of the confluence of the rivers. In the meantime, such poor quarters as he could provide for the night and such food as the resources of his village could furnish, were at their disposal. Nevertheless, it gradually dawned upon Denne that his host had something on his mind; he kept hanging around with the air of a man trying to arrive at a decision. At long last, when his guests had eaten their frugal dinner and were just settling down to rest, he intimated that he had a question to ask.

"As a mere matter of curiosity, sahib, supposing by some chance you had come upon these dangerous ruffians whom you have been pursuing—supposing you could have taken them quite by surprise, perhaps asleep round their camp fires—what exactly would you have done? You see you have very few men with you?"

"Offered them one chance of surrendering, and shot them down if they did not do so immediately," was the reply.

"Is that really so?" said the landholder. "I thought you would be obliged to try and capture them alive; you could never do that—there is not the slightest chance of their surrendering. Then, when they had got away, the armed police cannot stay in my village for ever, and they would be terribly revenged on anyone who had betrayed their hiding place."

By this time Denne was growing interested. "What is the meaning of all this?" he asked. "Speak out, man: you have far more to fear from the English Government than you have from these desperate fugitives from justice."

"I will speak out," was the reply. "If you will really do what you say, if I may be assured of safety under the protection of the Government, I can take you straight to their camp; it is less than two miles from here. May I be forgiven, but they have used awful threats; I was afraid to tell you this at first. And you and your men were very weary when you arrived here—also hungry. It seemed right to me that you should have food and rest."

A little later Denne needed all his self-control before he could settle down to a quiet discussion with a group of villagers, now desperately eager to atone for the consequences of their timidity and hesitation, as to the next move in the game. He had reached the dacoit camp about a couple of hours too late. The fires at which they had cooked their evening meal were still burning; but they had moved on.

By daybreak the pursuit was taken up, with a force augmented by a sub-inspector of police summoned from the nearest outpost, a handful of village watchmen with their iron-bound quarter-staffs, two or three landholders from the neighbourhood, and a couple of expert trackers who vowed that if they had nothing else to go by but the hoof-marks of the horse the dacoits had lifted from Ujhani Police Station, that was a trail they could follow to the world's end. They were as good as their word, for somewhere about eleven o'clock that morning, riding with the local sub-inspector along a rough track through the scrub jungle, Denne was fired upon by two of the men guarding the rear of the outlaws. It was here that the personality of Dhara Singh asserted itself. An ordinary dacoit gang would have broken up and scattered, but he managed to keep his men in hand, fighting a rear-guard action which held the pursuers off for a couple of hours. The dacoits abandoned most of their scanty baggage as they went, including some bundles of miscellaneous loot, one of which proved to contain the fair

Shahzadi's zither; but their leader must gradually have arrived at an accurate estimate of the size of the force against him and begun to look out for some position where he could make a stand. When the police party emerged into open country near the river-bank they found they had brought their quarry to bay, but that it was going to prove an awkward animal to tackle.

Close at hand lay a little cluster of thatched huts forming the hamlet of Panjab Nagla. Some distance from the rest, on a bluff overlooking the bed of the Ramgunga River, stood a house, or rather a walled enclosure, evidently the residence of the most substantial family in the place. The courtyard had only one entrance-door, low and narrow; three or four sheds and two flat-roofed houses stood in the enclosure. Along one side the outer wall was little more than breast-high, a convenient rampart to be held by resolute men with firearms in their hands and a good supply of ammunition. For an attack on such a position the peasants and village watchmen who had joined Denne's force were useless; he could reckon only on one head-constable and six men of the armed police and the sub-inspector of the civil police. He was outnumbered by just about three to one. It was soon evident, moreover, that for the purposes of an encounter under existing conditions the dacoits were more efficiently armed than their assailants. Denne had expended some cartridges in keeping his enemy on the run during the morning; his own ammunition was soon reduced to the cartridges loaded with snipe-shot which he found in his belt, and the problem was to get to close enough quarters to make snipe-shot effective. The armed police carried ancient Sniders discarded from the army when the Martini-Henry rifle came into use; with their worn-out rifling and indifferent ammunition they could not be relied on to hit a barn door at thirty yards. The dacoits were firing slugs from shot-guns and bell-mouthed blunderbusses; their position could only be reached by a rush across the open of nowhere less than thirty yards.

Dhara Singh organised his defence skilfully. Two of his most reliable men he bound by an oath, taken across a bowl of Ganges water, to fire at no one except 'the sahib,' who must necessarily take the lead in any attempt to rush the enclosure. He defeated an attempt to fire the thatched huts by hacking down from the inside the supports of the thatched roofs and stacking all the inflammable material well inside the courtyard. In the encounter that followed the honours of the first round went entirely to the dacoits. Denne managed to lead a little group of his men as far as the last available piece of cover, a low wall on the edge of the village separated by some thirty yards of open ground from the enclosure held by the dacoits. He remembered some time later that on the way there he had turned and roundly cursed the two constables behind him for firing wildly in the air; the subconscious reason for his irritation was that one of them had shot him through the fleshy part of the left shoulder, missing the bone by a very little. As he rose to his feet behind the low wall he found himself covered by the muzzle of a weapon levelled over the top of the rampart opposite. He threw his gun to his shoulder and the two reports rang out simultaneously. Denne was quite a good snipe-shot; he himself stopped two slugs with his left forearm, but the dacoit dropped. About the same moment the constable nearest to Denne, a burly Sikh—a man reserved by fate for a tragic end, of which I have something to tell later,—was disabled by a nasty wound in the right shoulder. To make matters worse, Head Constable Amir-ullah, who had been told off to lead a small party to a point from which he was to head a charge if a favourable opportunity offered, was taken with a fit of berserker madness. Alone and unsupported he raced across the open and had one hand on the enclosure wall when Pohpi Singh stepped forward and shot him dead, his gun-muzzle almost touching the man's temple. Denne withdrew his men out of range and made no further attack.

The position was not one calling for desperate measures. As soon as Denne established contact with the dacoits he had sent off runners with the news. Reinforcements were soon on their way, not only armed police from Budaun but a detachment of lancers from the Indian Cavalry regiment at Bareilly. If the dacoits elected to remain where they were their capture was a certainty; the first question, therefore, was whether they could be bluffed into doing so. On the other hand, it was probable that they would follow their usual custom of making a night march, and it remained to be seen whether they could do this without laying themselves open to attack. The river in their rear was unfordable and they had no boats; this simplified the problem, but Denne's available forces were still quite inadequate for an effective blockade. Collecting every able-bodied man available, putting each group in charge of some responsible person and assigning at least one firearm to each, he managed to form a rough cordon of posts, hemming his opponents in and commanding every track or footpath they might be expected to follow if they made for the jungle. He himself, with two constables of the armed police, lay in ambush at a point where they had the shelter of a bamboo clump and the earthen boundary of a small orchard, but could command a well-defined track leading through the village lands into the scrub.

It was the night of the November full moon; Dhara Singh waited until it was high in the heavens, got his men together, and marched them out in an irregular column with the mounted men mostly at the head. As it happened he walked straight into the snare which had been set for him. With one exception the little groups of the blockading cordon were advertising their presence with lighted fires and loud talk, perhaps with a view to impressing the enemy or possibly to keep up their own spirits. Denne himself and his two constables were well hidden and kept perfectly still. Dhara Singh may have thought that this particular line of retreat was unguarded; at any rate he took it. As the column came abreast of their ambush the three policemen fired; two of the dacoits fell, one dead and the other dying. This sudden volley out of the darkness was too much for the nerves and the still imperfect discipline of the dacoit gang; they not only broke and fled, but they scattered. They were never together again as an organised body.

There was no pursuit beyond what was necessary to make certain of the rout, and only one more prisoner was taken that night. When the police entered the enclosure where the dacoits had made their stand, they found first of all one dead man; his face was pitted with pellets of snipe-shot and both eyes had been pierced. Further search disclosed, hidden under a heap of thatch, one wretched coward whose heart had failed him so that he slunk back into shelter when the rest marched out. When discovered he cringed and entreated. He was ready with a full list of the gang and a detailed story of their doings for the past fortnight; he begged to be taken before a Magistrate that his confession might be recorded—anything, in short, for the chance of turning Queen's Evidence, that he might appear at the trial in the witness-box and not in the dock.

The three leaders of the gang and perhaps half a dozen of their trustiest followers managed to keep together in the flight. They must have gone through adventures the details of which I never learnt. They managed to recross the Ganges into the Etah District; rumour had it that they seized some village buffaloes, drove them into the stream and got across by holding on to the beasts as they swam. For some precarious weeks they evaded arrest, but the end was inevitable. Their lurking-place was betrayed to the Etah police and they were cornered by superior forces. Even then they fought as long as Dhara Singh was alive to lead them. When he fell, shot through the spine as he stooped over a wounded comrade, the survivors dropped their weapons and surrendered.

CHAPTER VI.

THE ARM OF THE LAW.

THE procedure followed by the Indian Courts in dealing with an important case like that now initiated against Pohpi Singh and his fellow-accused may require some little explanation for English readers. To begin with, one stage which takes up a great deal of time in England is practically eliminated. I mean the inquest before the coroner. It is true that a paper will appear on the Indian record which is usually referred to as the 'inquest report,' but this is merely a formal examination of the dead body by the police officer charged with the investigation, in the presence of certain villagers who act as a jury and certify to the presence or absence of marks of injury. The post-mortem examination will be conducted by the Civil Surgeon; there is as a rule only one such official in an Indian district and his time is valuable. His deposition will be recorded by the Magistrate conducting the preliminary inquiry in the presence of the accused, who will be offered an opportunity of cross-examining. The deposition so recorded is admissible in evidence at the subsequent trial, without the attendance of the Civil Surgeon being required unless he is specially summoned by the Judge for further examination.

The proceedings before the Magistrate are important; his functions are wider than those of an English Magistrate, approximating in some respects to those of a French 'Juge d'Instruction.' Broadly speaking, it is his duty to see that the case for the prosecution is completely prepared for presentation to the trial Court. He has large powers in the matter of summoning additional evidence over and above that tendered by the police. He is required to question the accused in order to afford the latter an opportunity of contesting, commenting upon or explaining the evidence against him, though the accused is not placed upon oath, is not subject to cross-examination, and indeed is at liberty to decline to answer any or every question put to him. The Magistrate is required to call upon the accused to put in a list of all witnesses whom he desires to have summoned in his defence; if he desires to keep the names of his witnesses secret he can do so at the risk of their putting in an appearance at the trial voluntarily without process of Court. At the conclusion of his proceedings the Magistrate has not merely to draw up a 'commital order' in which he sets forth the substance of the evidence given in his court with such comments as he may think proper, but he prepares for the assistance of the Sessions Judge a formal 'calendar,' containing the names of the prosecution witnesses with the nature of the evidence given by each, the names of the witnesses summoned for the defence, and other matters calculated to facilitate proceedings at the trial. It may be said in a general way that the Indian Code of Criminal Procedure seeks to supplement the presumed inadequacy of the prosecuting agency, especially in outlying districts, by throwing a great deal of work and responsibility on the 'Committing Magistrate,' who nevertheless remains a judicial officer, bound by all the rules of evidence, and entitled even to discharge the accused person if the result of his proceedings is to demonstrate that there is no case against him deserving consideration by the Judge.

The trial in the 'Court of Session' will be before a Judge, sitting without a jury and bound to give his own decision on every question of fact or of law. The jury system is still in its infancy in Northern India, being limited to trials before the High Courts, and in respect of certain classes of offences before Sessions Judges exercising jurisdiction in a few of the large towns. In other cases the Judge has the assistance of two or more 'Assessors,' chosen very much as jurymen are in England, whose opinions he is bound to record and consider, but not to adopt unless he holds them to be correct. I have always understood that the main object of this system of trial "with the aid of Assessors" was to train certain classes of the population in the exercise of functions approximating to those of a jury, and so to pave the way for the gradual extension of the jury system. If so, singularly little progress has been made in this direction in my time, or will be until something is done to instil a sense of genuine responsibility into the Assessors, as, for instance, by providing that there shall be no appeal on the facts where the Sessions Judge accepts and endorses the unanimous opinion of the Assessors. I was a little surprised to find, on one occasion when I was in a position to press for an amendment of the law in this direction, that opposition came from the representatives of educated Indian opinion. It would seem that, in the opinion of Indian lawyers at any rate, security for life and liberty is better guaranteed by the existing system than it would be by any extension of power to the still imperfectly educated classes from which jurymen would have to be drawn.

The working substitute for trial by jury may be fairly described as one of retrial upon the record. An appeal on questions of fact as well as of law lies to the High Court of the Province against every conviction at a trial held by a Sessions Judge sitting with Assessors; a corresponding right of appeal is allowed to the Local Government against acquittals so recorded. All Government appeals, and all appeals against a sentence of death or of transportation for life, are heard in the High Court by a Bench of two Judges. Moreover, where the trial Judge has passed sentence of death, he must refer the case to the High Court for confirmation; this means that, even if there is no appeal, no capital sentence will be carried out until two Judges of the High Court have examined the record and satisfied themselves that the conviction and the sentence are warranted in fact and in law. The warrants of execution in capital cases are sent down over the signatures of the Judges of the High Court.

In the present instance the duties and responsibilities of 'Committing Magistrate' fell to my lot, and they were no light burden. The evidence to be sifted and arranged covered a wide field; a great deal of it consisted of the statements of witnesses not previously acquainted with any of the accused and who had seen them but once. It had to be carefully considered what legal proof there was of the association of each of the accused men with the rest, and of his individual complicity in the acts alleged. Eventually I drew up three 'charges,' as they are called in India, upon which the accused were to be tried. The first, intended to link up the converging threads of the evidence, was that each and all of them, between specified dates and at various places within my jurisdiction, had belonged to a gang of persons associated for the purpose of habitually committing dacoity. The second related to the dacoity at Laindheri and the murder of Sahbi Singh. The third was with reference to the encounter with the police and the murder of Head Constable Amirullah.

As the proceedings in my Court continued I became increasingly interested in the personality of the two surviving brothers. Bijai Singh preserved throughout a dreamy, abstracted air and an almost impenetrable silence. Pohpi Singh took the defence of himself and his fellows almost entirely out of the hands of the lawyers, fighting every point of the game with dogged pertinacity and invincible good-humour. Not for one instant did he swerve from the position that he and his brother were respectable landholders, harried out of house and home by the oppression of corrupt police officers, who were now producing perjured evidence to implicate them in the doings of a gang of desperate ruffians whom they had never seen or heard of until they listened with interest and amazement to the stories of the said witnesses.

"Really, Pohpi Singh," I said to him at the termination of one day's proceedings, "it does seem a pity that you could not find better employment for your talents. If you had only joined the police, now, just think what a Prosecuting Inspector you would have made!" He laughed quite cheerfully: "You are right there, sahib," he said, "so I should."

One little trap he laid for me which I had some difficulty in evading. When the list of witnesses was handed in whom he desired to have summoned for the defence of himself and his co-accused, I found amongst them the name of Mr Justice Aikman of the Allahabad High Court; he was to prove that on one of the crucial dates in the case Pohpi Singh had appeared personally to present a petition before that learned Judge in his Court. Now I knew, and I have no doubt Pohpi Singh also knew, that Mr Justice (afterwards Sir Robert) Aikman had recently left India for England on a well-earned furlough. What precisely the defence hoped to gain by this move I cannot say, possibly they hoped for a lengthy postponement of the trial and the chance of corrupting or intimidating some of the prosecution witnesses. On the whole, however, I think the idea was simply to play out the game according to its rules and score every point which those rules allowed. It would have been open to me to grant the application with the proviso that the accused must, in so exceptional a case, deposit a sum sufficient to cover the travelling expenses of the witness. I thought over this alternative, and very foolish I should have looked if I had adopted it. I learnt afterwards that the accused had five thousand rupees ready in cash outside the Court, to be handed in if any deposit should be required. As it happened, I elected to put a few questions to Pohpi Singh personally on his application. He had been imperfectly coached in respect of the correspondence between the English date mentioned in his petition and the Hindu calendar for the month ; it soon came out that his application involved the assertion that he had personally tendered a petition in the Allahabad High Court on a day on which that Court was not sitting. I rejected the application, in so far as it related to Mr Justice Aikman, as one presented merely " for vexation and delay and to defeat the ends of justice." I am not particularly proud of my action in this matter, but, of course, it was preposterous on the face of it to suppose that a Judge of the High Court could recognise the features of a litigant who had tendered a petition to him some months previously. Certainly, Pohpi Singh himself never bore me the least grudge in the matter; I have no doubt he thought that I, too, was playing the very curious game of the English Law Courts according to its rules.

When it came to the trial before the Sessions Judge, the fact that the accused had ample funds at their disposal was emphasised by the appearance of the leader of the English Bar from Allahabad to conduct the defence. He began by claiming a separate trial on each of the three charges. The plea would have seriously embarrassed the prosecution if it had succeeded. It was a very arguable one; indeed, I will go so far as to say that I should have felt considerable difficulty thirty years later in supporting the procedure for which I had, as Joint Magistrate, made myself responsible. However, it was overruled, and on the facts the case gradually developed by the prosecution evidence was an overwhelming one. The Judge found all the accused guilty, and sent up the record to the High Court for confirmation of the sentences of death passed by him; the accused also exercised their right of appeal.

An interval of some weeks followed. In my time the Allahabad High Court has been at great pains to expedite in every possible way the hearing of appeals and references in capital cases. Thirty-five years ago these matters were dealt with in accordance with a leisurely routine which often left an interval of six weeks or more between the passing of a sentence of death and its confirmation by the superior Court. During the interval which ensued in this particular case, the Civil Surgeon of Budaun took a short spell of leave, his duties as Jail Superintendent were passed on for the time being to that maid-of-all-work, the Joint Magistrate of the district.

Thus it was that I found myself, morning after morning, making a formal round of jail inspection while Pohpi Singh and his fellows were lying in the condemned cells. I had imagination enough to realise the deadly monotony in which their days were passed, and I made a point of stopping for half an hour or so each morning to talk with them and with Pohpi Singh in particular. I really got to know him during those days, and I learnt much from him. That my kindness of intention was understood and appreciated I received proof one morning when I arrived an hour or so behind my usual time; they were unquestionably glad to see me, and relieved that my tardy appearance did not mean that I had discontinued my visits.

As a matter of fact I was bringing news that day. I had been obliged to attend an early morning parade at which the District Magistrate had distributed the rewards, formally sanctioned after the inevitable delay and expenditure of red-tape, for those members of the police force who had distinguished themselves in Mr Denne's encounter with the gang. Pohpi Singh could not conceal his interest; he was commenting freely on the amount and distribution of the rewards before he recollected himself sufficiently to explain that the story of the affair, as told by the witnesses at the trial, had impressed him so deeply that he realised it as vividly as if he had been actually present. One little item of my news I purposely kept back, expecting a question, which my reticence at last extorted. "It was said," remarked Pohpi Singh, slowly choosing his words, "that one man, a Mohammedan, a big man, displayed great courage. He, unhappily, was killed: even the Government (he smiled faintly) could not reward him. Is it not so?" "That is true, Pohpi Singh," I replied, "but it pleases me that you have asked about this. The widow of Head Constable Amirullah has received a special grant of three hundred rupees." He drew a long breath. "That is very right and proper; that is good news," he said. We looked hard at one another and I left him.

For the doomed men the end came in due course. The red warrants arrived from the High Court; all the appeals had been dismissed and the sentences confirmed. The Civil Surgeon had returned from leave and resumed charge of the jail, so that it did not fall to me to take the news to the condemned cells, but the superintendence of the executions was one of my miscellaneous duties as Joint Magistrate. Four men were to suffer that first morning: Pohpi Singh, Bijai Singh, Komil Singh, and Bhawan. Our apparatus was a little primitive and we had to hang them in pairs, with due observance of the prescribed interval of three-quarters of an hour between the executions. In the early grey of a May morning the small company gathered in the jail yard, Fischer and myself, a guard of the armed police, two or three nervous and fidgety jail officials, the executioner and his menials. Outside the enclosure, but so placed as to be able to command a view of the proceedings over a low wall, gathered a group of spectators. In my time, at any rate, executions were carried out in view of the public, not for the sake of example but to meet the danger that the wildest rumours might otherwise gain credence as to the methods employed.

While all the convicts met their fate with resolution, the wrestler, Bhawan, the man whose reckless savagery had fixed the noose round the necks of all of them, displayed a certain insolent bravado. "I have a petition to make!" he cried at the gallows' foot; "I desire to go through my exercises once more before I die!" I looked keenly at him. "See here, Bhawan," I said, "if this is some trick, it is quite useless. These men here have their guns loaded and will fire if I give the signal." "It is no trick, sahib," he replied, "I know that in five minutes' time I shall be hanged and dead, but I want to go through my exercises once again." "Loose him," I commanded, and in the centre of the staring group he went rapidly through the Sandow exercises with which Indian wrestlers keep their muscles in condition. As he rose to his feet on their conclusion he smote himself violently on the chest. "It is now time," he cried loudly, ran up the steps of the gallows and struck an attitude at the top. He was almost peevish at being compelled to abandon it, because the regulations required that he should die with his arms pinioned, his feet bound together, and a cap drawn over his face.

The two brothers had suffered first. From the moment they stepped into the little courtyard Pohpi Singh had only one anxiety: of himself he was quite sure, but whatever else happened his younger brother must not show the white feather. There was a ghastly little hitch over the unfastening of their handcuffs—the keys would not turn until the locks had been oiled. Pohpi Singh was the least concerned of those present. "Put your arms straight out, like this," he said to his brother, "how can you expect the key to turn if you go moving them about?" And Bijai Singh stiffened his shaking arms. They walked up the ladder side by side, and the level rays of the rising sun caught their faces as they cleared the height of the jail wall. Both swung round towards it, calling on the name of their God, the hero of Tulsi Das's immortal epic, that Bible of Northern India, the story of a God who was made man, and suffered for the good of human kind. "Ram! Ram! Ram!" they chanted. As the executioner came behind them to make his last preparations, Pohpi Singh motioned him back a moment. Looking out over our heads to the little knot of spectators, he called in a loud voice, "Listen, everyone here! We ask to be forgiven for whatever of wrong we have committed"—and he resumed the monotonous chant. For one moment Bijai Singh's voice faltered, and there was a little quiver about his knees. "Call on Rama!" said his brother sternly, and once more their voices rose together, "Ram! Ram! Ram!" The executioner stepped back off the platform, a rope was pulled—and their case had gone up to a Higher Court.

CHAPTER VII.

A TAIL-PIECE.

THE irruption of this gang of outlaws into the Budaun District produced after-effects like the ripples following upon the fall of a large stone into a still pool. By way of appendix to my story I have something to add about certain of these.

I am glad that Pohpi Singh never knew what followed upon the grant of three hundred rupees to the widow of Head Constable Amirullah. One morning some weeks later, I received the somewhat unusual message that a woman was in the verandah of my house asking to see me. When admitted to my office she proved to be the Head Constable's mother, and she fell at my feet in a passion of entreaty that a benign Government might be pleased to take back this fatal gift. She was very fond of her daughter-in-law, whom she described as young, handsome, self-willed, and utterly without experience of the world. She was now being courted by the biggest blackguard in the neighbourhood. He did not care a button for her; once married he would coax her out of the money, squander it all in a month's dissipation, and make her miserable for the rest of her life. He was a notorious drunkard and gambler, but the young widow had conceived an infatuation for him and would listen to no advice. I am afraid the little advice I could give was no more effective: as for the money, it had been paid over—and "the gods themselves cannot recall their gifts."

There was another curious little episode of which I never heard the final outcome. The police had in their hands a complete list of the men who had been with Pohpi Singh and his brothers during their march across the Budaun District, and those not yet accounted for were being hunted down one by one. The Criminal Procedure Code provides for the attachment, under a Magistrate's warrant, of the property of an offender who has absconded to avoid arrest; but most of this work was being done in this instance by the Magistrate on the Etah side of the river. I received, however, a formal report from one of my Police Inspectors, asking for such a warrant in respect of one, Baldeo Singh, described as a resident of an out-of-the-way village near the Ganges on my side of the river. The name was a common one but I seemed to have heard it before in connection with this case. I sent for the Inspector. "I don't understand this," I said. "Baldeo Singh was the man found dead in the enclosure, the man whom the Superintendent Sahib had shot all over the face. You cannot attach the property of a dead man as that of an absconding offender." "I know that, Sahib," was the reply, " but there is something very queer about this matter. Of course, the face of the dead man was quite unrecognisable, but the man who gave us the list of the gang mentioned Baldeo Singh as having been shot in the face by the Superintendent Sahib, and we entered the name accordingly. Since then we have heard from the Etah police that a man of another name, whom they have got on their list of absconders, has never returned to his village and the members of his family say they are certain he was killed in the fight with the police. This caused us to make further inquiries about Baldeo Singh. One thing is quite certain, his wife has not put off her ornaments as she would have done if she believed herself to be a widow. Nor is she being treated as a widow by the rest of the family. We told off an informer to keep secret watch on Baldeo Singh's house, and he came to the police station two days ago with a very strange story. Baldeo Singh had a daughter married some time back, but not yet made over to her husband. The bridegroom's family sent to fetch her last week, and our informer says that Baldeo Singh was brought secretly to the house by night to be present at the ceremonies connected with the departure of the bride. He was brought there, Sahib, because he is quite blind, though they are keeping him in hiding somewhere in the waste lands along the river. Now, we know that Denne Sahib fired not one shot only, but several, from his gun in the course of the encounter: what wonder if he succeeded in hitting two of the dacoits in the face? If this information is true he must have done so, and Baldeo Singh must have been led away on the back of a horse when the dacoits left the enclosure."

I signed the warrant, but I heard no more except that the property seized as Baldeo Singh's under the order of attachment proved to be of trifling value. So far as I know Baldeo Singh was never arrested, but the idea of the blinded outlaw, supported in some secret hiding-place and smuggled into his house by night to give a father's blessing to the departing bride, has haunted my memory.

It remains to tell of the tragic end of Mahpal Singh, the constable who was wounded at Denne's side during his skirmish. He was a Sikh from the Panjab, a strapping fellow who might have found his way into the army if he had not belonged to the very lowest order of his community, and it may be also if he had not been a densely stupid person. The armed police force often picks up men who are not quite good enough for the army. The psychological effect on this man of having been paraded before the District Magistrate, to listen to a warm encomium of his courage and good conduct, and to receive a handsome pecuniary reward, was entirely disastrous. The police lines were not big enough to hold him; he swaggered about the bazaar at all hours, absenting himself from duty whenever he felt so inclined, and receiving with insolence the rebukes or punishments he thereby incurred. Denne was reluctant to deal severely with the man and hoped that a spell of quiet monotony might give him a chance to settle down and reduce the swelled head from which he was obviously suffering. He transferred him for duty as one of the guards over the sub-treasury at Gunnaur, in a lonely corner of the district far removed from such temptations as were to be found in the Budaun bazaar. There, however, matters went from bad to worse, for Constable Mahpal Singh proceeded to seek adventure in his own way. The *Tahsildar*—the Revenue Officer and Subordinate Magistrate—at Gunnaur was a Mohammedan of good family, punctilious in his religious observances. Mahpal Singh apparently resented some efforts on the part of this officer to keep him in order; he corrupted another member of the guard who was a co-religionist of his own, and the two of them started a campaign of annoyance against the *Tahsildar* by blowing loudly upon a conch at all his hours of prayer. When threatened with punishment for this they retorted with insolence, and Mahpal Singh fired a shot in at the gateway of the *Tahsildar's* private quarters, presumably as a gesture of supreme contempt. He was summoned back to Budaun and placed under detention in the police lines, pending a formal inquiry into his conduct.

That inquiry was never completed. There happened to be living in an outlying part of the city of Budaun a man of the name of Shakru, a carpenter by trade, an under-sized, timid, and utterly inoffensive creature. Shakru had a wife much sturdier than himself in character as in person, a fine figure of a woman. I do not know with certainty when or how she first attracted the favourable notice of Constable Mahpal Singh, but there had been an intrigue between them before the latter left for Gunnaur. The woman must not be judged too harshly. Her husband was a worm of a man; this great, burly, swaggering Sikh came into her life with the glamour upon him of approved heroism in fight, as a very incarnation of romance in her drab existence. I heard later that she bore a son whose father was undoubtedly Mahpal Singh, and I could fancy that son in later years speaking of his mother's lapse from duty much in the style of the Bastard Faulconbridge to his mother.

When Mahpal Singh got back from Gunnaur the situation became intolerable. Lover and mistress discarded all pretence at concealment. Mahpal Singh was nominally confined to the police barracks, but he contrived somehow or other to spend a good part of each day in Shakru's enclosure, treating the wretched little carpenter with open derision.

There came an evening when Shakru, returning from a job of work with a bag of tools over his shoulder, reached the cross-roads in the heart of the city. There Mahpal Singh was standing in conversation with some friends. His eye caught the carpenter stealing inoffensively past along the side-walk: looking over his shoulder and pointing the man out to his friends, he launched some ultimate insult in that direction and turned his back with a roar of laughter. Something must have snapped inside the little man's head. Quite deliberately he set down his bundle on the kerb, unfastened it, selected a long-handled adze and walked towards his enemy. With a full swing of his implement, rising on his toes to do it, the little man brought the sharp edge of the adze crashing in where the folds of the voluminous Sikh turban just failed to cover the back of the neck. The burly sepoy fell like a log. There was no need for a second blow, but for a minute or so the little man saw red. Kicking the turban to one side he struck again and yet again, until mere pieces and fragments of a shattered head lay on the hard road before him. Not one of the bystanders laid a finger on him. With set face he walked away down the street to the central Police Station, perhaps a couple of hundred yards distant. He turned in at the gate, marched up to the table where the clerk on duty sat recording the day's reports, flung the dripping adze down at the man's feet and remarked, "I have killed Police Constable Mahpal Singh; you can arrange about my hanging."

When they brought Shakru into my court next day the hot fit was over; I saw before me a little man, frightened and cringing, weeping hysterical tears, stammering out incredible and incoherent denials. I sent him up for trial on a charge of "culpable homicide not amounting to murder," taking it on myself to hold that there had been sufficient "grave and sudden provocation" to extenuate the offence, at least to this extent. I believe he received quite a light sentence.

PART II.

LEAVES FROM MY CASE-BOOK

I.

ONE FROM JUDGE JEFFREYS' BOOK.

SOME years back it fell to my lot to place my wider experience in the matter at the disposal of an American tourist, a railway magnate in his own country, who was seeing the sights of Florence. We were walking home after a long day in the great picture galleries, when he emerged from a reverie to ask me whether he might take it that the numerous portraits which we had passed in review had been painted from their living subjects. On being assured that this was so, " And what did they do to the painters ? " he inquired.

I replied that they held them in great honour and rewarded them munificently.

He shook his head : " They must have been a very forgiving people," he remarked.

" I'm afraid I don't get you," was my reply.

" Well," said he, " in my line of business you don't get very far unless you learn to be something of a physiognomist. Now, I was thinking over all these faces we have seen to-day, popes and cardinals and grand-dukes and other great men in their day : there was not one of those faces the owner of which I would have trusted with a five-dollar bill."

This episode recurred to my mind as I sat in Room No. VIII. of the National Portrait Gallery considering the picture of George, first Lord Jeffreys. The inscription at the foot tells you that it was painted while its subject was still Recorder of London; he was, therefore, between thirty and thirty-five years of age, and neither so great nor so terrible a personage as he became during the last six years of his short life. Presumably, however, the painter intended to produce a likeness which would please his sitter, and I am prepared to believe that he succeeded. At first sight, indeed, the portrait has caused a shock of surprise to everyone who has come upon it unexpectedly, with previous knowledge of the reputation earned by Judge Jeffreys of the "Bloody Assize." The face is a distinctly handsome one, with something about it that suggests an artist or a poet. This I knew beforehand; the object of my visit was to examine the picture minutely in detail.

I began with the hands; these are often merely conventional, but when studied from life they can be very instructive. There is a portrait at Oxford of King Henry V. in which the hands have been very carefully painted; and a doctor who knew what he was talking about pronounced them to be, beyond question, the hands of a consumptive. In the Jeffreys portrait the long fingers with their filbert nails seem appropriate to the artistic temperament suggested by the face, but there is something odd about the left thumb. Either that hand has been badly drawn or the thumb is that of a man suffering from arthritis.

The eyes fairly puzzled me. My own experience suggests that innate cruelty of disposition goes with grey or steely blue eyes; Jeffreys was undoubtedly a cruel man, one who delighted in the infliction of suffering and humiliation, but his eyes are a rich deep brown. Over their expression I pondered for some time, and I can only record my own belief that the man whose eyes, when in repose, had that look in them was aware, subconsciously, that he would never live to see old age. The corners are blood-shot; the man was not yet a drunkard but he was drinking hard.

The character of the face, at first sight, is dominated by the splendid nose, the eyebrows, and the forehead, but when one follows the line of the nose down to the mouth one begins to realise the man. The marked indentation down the centre of the upper lip does not keep the line of the nose; the mouth is slewed round to the right, and the right nostril curves. The under lip protrudes slightly, the mouth as a whole suggesting both cynicism and sensuality. I could see the grim smile and the terror looking out of the eyes as he recommended the unlucky adventuress whom he had just sentenced to the cart's tail to the "special attention" of the hangman. "Scourge her soundly, man, scourge her till the blood runs down. It is Christmas, cold weather for madam to strip in; see that you warm her shoulders thoroughly." The words were not shouted, they were spoken with slow relish, in an even tone, the eyes gloating over the white face of the victim.

Having recorded this impression I feel that I run a considerable risk of discrediting myself in the eyes of my readers by undertaking, first, to say a few words in defence of Judge Jeffreys' conduct of a certain famous trial, and further to describe an occasion on which I quite consciously and deliberately took a leaf out of his book. Before coming to this, however, I take leave to interpose a brief digression on a point of literary criticism which has intrigued me a good deal. I have always understood that the account of the trial of Faithful at Vanity Fair entitled John Bunyan to a high position in the roll of English satirists; it certainly reads like a bitter attack on the conduct of political trials in Bunyan's time. Now, at Vanity Fair "the judge's name was Lord Hate-good"; his comments on the prosecution evidence, his frank abuse of the prisoner at the bar, and his summing-up to the jury are all quite extraordinarily like certain accounts which have come down to us of the behaviour of Judge Jeffreys on similar occasions. There is an eloquent passage somewhere in Macaulay which calls attention to the likeness between this trial and one held in a court "where all the vices sat enthroned" in the person of Chief Justice Jeffreys. Personally I took it for granted that a character sketch of the cruel Judge, from the point of view of the greatest writer of the class which suffered most at his hands, was obviously intended. The trouble is that the dates will not fit. 'The Pilgrim's Progress' was published in 1678, the year in which Jeffreys became Recorder of London; the eighth edition, containing the last additions and improvements made by the author himself, came out in 1682, the year before Jeffreys was promoted to Lord Chief Justice. I should very much like to know if the account of the trial, and particularly the picture of my Lord Hate-good, was in any way amplified or touched up by the author in the interval between the first and the eighth editions; but it is intrinsically improbable that Bunyan should have anticipated the promotion or the repute subsequently gained by Lord Jeffreys. I am tempted, indeed, to look at the coincidence from an opposite angle. The accounts which have come down to us of Jeffreys' behaviour at the trial of Richard Baxter, and on various occasions during the Bloody Assize, are partisan accounts written undoubtedly by the sort of people who would have read 'The Pilgrim's Progress': is it conceivable that their presentment of Judge Jeffreys has been coloured by reminiscences of Lord Hate-good?

The particular trial to which I now turn my attention was that of Alice Lisle, held at Winchester in the month of August 1685, before Jeffreys as Lord Chief Justice. The charge against the prisoner was that she had been guilty of high treason, in that she had received and sheltered in her house for a single night, one John Hickes, a Nonconformist minister, he being at the time a fugitive rebel from the army of the Duke of Monmouth which had been defeated and scattered at Sedgemoor a fortnight before. Now, it is no part of my brief—if I may be allowed the expression—to defend the action of the Government which claimed the grim penalties of high treason from an old lady of seventy for an act of womanly mercy, but even here there is something to be said. As I read the history of the time, the Government of King James II. had been badly shaken by Monmouth's rebellion, much more so than we who read the story with foreknowledge of the event can readily conceive. The plain truth is that we do not know who was and who was not ready to declare himself on Monmouth's side if the night attack on the royalist camp at Sedgemoor had succeeded. The savage measures of repression which followed were in part the result of panic. It may be added that they were singularly effective, as William of Orange was to discover when he landed at Torbay three years later. The Whigs of the West country hung back, panic-stricken; the monarchy of James II. only fell when the Tory Earl of Danby had roused the North against him, and Churchill's defection had taken all the fight out of his army.

Moreover, Alice Lisle was a person of some importance. Her late husband, John Lisle, had been one of the judges at the trial of Charles I., a fact not to be easily forgotten in those days. He was also a member of Cromwell's House of

Lords, and his widow was commonly spoken of as 'Lady Lisle' amongst her neighbours. She was a professed royalist, but her leanings towards the Protestant Dissenters were well known, and Monmouth's rebellion had been in the main a rising of the Dissenters. Without labouring the point further, I have no doubt the Crown lawyers in London, who instituted the prosecution, congratulated themselves on being able to initiate their campaign of terror by making it clear that underhand sympathy with Dissent on the part of influential persons, professedly loyal to the established government in Church and State, was peculiarly heinous in their eyes.

The case, however, was not being tried in London but in Hampshire, before a jury of country gentlemen who, if not personally acquainted with the prisoner, knew her well enough by name and reputation. Nothing could persuade them that the gentle and inoffensive old lady in the dock was really a dangerous traitor, even supposing she had permitted herself, out of womanly kindness and respect for the memory of her dead husband, to shelter a despairing fugitive belonging to his party in politics and religion. As honest English gentlemen they respected the oath they had taken to return a true verdict upon the evidence. One can imagine the feelings with which they listened to the Lord Chief Justice laying down the law; I quote the following passage at length, because it is really more characteristic of the way in which Jeffreys handled the case as a whole, than those sensational episodes which have given it notoriety.

> "And, gentlemen, I must tell you for law of which we are the judges and not you, that if any person be in actual rebellion against the King, and another person (who really and actually was not in rebellion) does receive, harbour, comfort, and conceal him that was such, a receiver is as much a traitor as he who indeed bore arms. We are bound by our oath and conscience to deliver and declare to you what is law; and you are bound by your oaths and consciences to deliver and declare to us, by your verdict, the truth of the fact."

The result of the trial proved that the gentlemen thus addressed, if driven into a corner from which they could find no loophole of escape, were prepared to discharge the duty laid upon them; but if there should prove to be a flaw in the prosecution case enabling them in honour and conscience to hold that the Crown had failed to establish by legal evidence one essential ingredient in the offence charged, happy would they be to find the prisoner 'not guilty.'

The defence set up by the prisoner seemed likely to provide the gentlemen of the jury with precisely the excuse for which they were seeking; it turned essentially upon a point peculiarly calculated to irritate as well as to embarrass the lawyers responsible for the prosecution. That John Hickes was in fact a fugitive rebel from Monmouth's army was clearly proved. It was also established that he had not merely been received and entertained in Lady Lisle's house, but that he had been quite definitely hidden there: he was brought to the house secretly at night, and his presence there was denied to the officers who came to search for him. It made matters worse that he was not alone, but in the company of one Richard Nelthorpe, who was under sentence of outlawry for having been concerned in a notorious assassination plot at the close of the previous reign. The Crown lawyers probably entered upon the trial in the belief that they had an easy case to prove: they were met by a defence which virtually admitted all the facts on which they relied, but pleaded that these were not sufficient for a conviction. It has been stated that Hickes was a Nonconformist minister; the prisoner asserted that she had received and concealed him in the belief that there were warrants out against him for preaching in contravention of the Conventicle Act. To put the point in her own words:—

> "But as for Mr Hickes I did not in the least suspect him to have been in the army, being a Presbyterian minister that used to preach and not to fight."

Now this defence was not in fact true; it was, indeed, a pretty thin one in view of the fact that the battle of Sedgemoor had been fought only two weeks before, and that fugitives from Monmouth's army were being hunted down all over the south-west of England. With a differently constituted jury, the prosecution might have been content to rely upon circumstantial evidence sufficient to render the prisoner's plea grossly improbable. As matters stood it was quite obvious that the jury intended to hold the Crown to strict proof of that guilty knowledge on the prisoner's part which alone could bring her offence within the law of high treason.

How was this proof to be supplied? What witnesses were available? Of the servants of the household, one Carpenter, described as the lady's 'bailiff,' had received the fugitives on their arrival and had served up the evening meal; this had been prepared by his wife. As far as Mr and Mrs Carpenter were concerned, any admission tending to incriminate their mistress had to be extorted from reluctant lips; moreover, it soon became apparent that whatever they may have known or suspected, they could protest with truth that nothing had been said in their presence as to the reason for Hickes and Nelthorpe seeking shelter and entertainment on the night in question.

There remained one possible witness, and one only. When the king's officers searched Lady Lisle's house they discovered, in addition to Hickes and Nelthorpe, an individual of the name of Dunne, "hiding in the malt-house." It was ascertained that Dunne had paid a preliminary visit to Lady Lisle the previous day in order to inquire whether she was willing to receive Hickes, and that he had returned after dark bringing both Hickes and Nelthorpe with him. The prosecution knew, moreover, that he had sat down to table with the mistress of the house and the two fugitives. The result of the trial turned on what Dunne was prepared to depose, or rather on how much of what he undoubtedly knew he could be induced to admit. The wretched man was, not unnaturally, in mortal terror lest he himself should be held to have overstepped the bounds of high treason by helping fugitive rebels to obtain an asylum. To do him justice, it must be added that his sympathies were wholly with the prisoner; it was horrible to him to realise that after he had presumed on the gentle lady's known tenderness of heart to induce her to break the law, he was called upon to speak the words that would consign her to a cruel doom. The point of the whole trial is that, after the prosecution lawyers had failed to obtain from Dunne any evidence sufficient for their purpose, the Chief Justice took the matter into his own hands and relentlessly extorted from the miserable witness what every soul in court knew to be the truth.

The modern reader may well ask what business this was of the Judge's. Should he not rather have sat austerely back in his seat of justice and watched with benevolent impartiality the prosecution breaking down on the dogged reticence of the witness and the sympathies of the jury? The only possible answer is that this was not the view of a Judge's duty which anyone at that time would have expected the Lord Chief Justice to take. The records of political trials held more than a hundred years later show that, in such cases, the presiding Judge held himself responsible for seeing that the case for the prosecution was fully and adequately presented to the jury, and was quite prepared to admonish wavering jurymen in no uncertain tone on their duty to King and country. In Jeffreys' time the position was even clearer; the Judges were His Majesty's Judges, removable from office at the King's pleasure, and very definitely expected to safeguard within the limits of established law the interests of the Crown. I do not overlook the fact that Jeffreys had already proved himself more than zealous in the royal service, or that he had gone down on his Western Assize under the special stimulus of a promise that the great prize of his profession, the Lord Chancellorship of England, might be earned by faithful and efficient service in what King James II. did not scruple to describe as the Lord Chief Justice's 'campaign' against the rebels.

Nevertheless, it cannot be denied that a more impartial judge than Jeffreys might well have been provoked by the palpable untruths and desperate equivocations of the witness; and if he is to be judged by the standards of his own time, it is hard to blame the Chief Justice for his grim resolve to get the truth out of the man before he had done with him. If this be conceded, it can only be said that his handling of the situation was masterly. Anyone reading Macaulay's account of the trial would suppose that he shouted and stormed and raved; the detailed report of the proceedings in the volume of the State Trials shows clearly enough that he did nothing of the sort. He was provoked to an outburst of indignation which sounds very unjudicial to modern ears by the prisoner's plea that she could not conceivably have supposed that a minister of religion like Hickes would have been in the ranks of Monmouth's army; but in his handling of Dunne I very much doubt if he raised his voice. His admonitions of the witness concerning the guilt of perjury and the peril of his immortal soul read to us very like cant, but it was an age in which men really believed that perjury was an offence against the Almighty. Moreover, Jeffreys understood the psychology of the case. He knew that a man will dare and endure much so long as he is convinced of the essential rightness of his conduct; it will be otherwise with one who is reduced to feeling himself upon a pinnacle of infamy, abhorred of God and despised by man. The crisis was reached in a curious way. Evidently the difficulties raised by the nature of the defence and the reluctance of the witnesses had prolonged the trial beyond expectations; lights were brought in. Suddenly the Judge turned to the Sheriff with the remark that he could no longer see the witness clearly enough. "Hold the candle to his face that we may see his brazen face." The order was obeyed; the wretched Dunne found himself standing, every eye in the crowded court fixed upon him, a dazzling light in his own eyes, and out of the darkness beyond, that grim relentless voice plying him with questions which fastened pitilessly upon every contradiction and evasion, extorted first one damaging admission and then another, brought him back continually to the essential point. The man broke down under the strain. He could not deny that he had in fact been served with supper in company of the prisoner and the two fugitives, that there had been conversation at table, and finally "that they talked of being in the army and of the fight."

It was repeatedly asserted afterwards by enemies of Jeffreys that the jury three times brought in the Lady Alice 'not guilty,' and that the Chief Justice refused to accept the verdict: this is not true. The jury returned to court three times, once to ask for a direction on a certain point of law, and twice to say that they felt a doubt whether it was fully proved that the prisoner knew that Hickes had been with the rebel army. The Chief Justice pressed them with the circumstantial evidence and the admission finally extorted from the miserable Dunne. In the end he told them that they must either agree upon a verdict or be locked up for the night: this also was made matter for complaint against him afterwards, but it was the invariable practice of the time. No one thought of objecting when it was followed, for instance, in the more famous trial of the Seven Bishops. The only verdict actually returned by the jury, at long last, was their hard-wrung, reluctant verdict of 'guilty.'

There are so many points of interest about this

trial that I am in danger of being carried far beyond my purpose in the attempt to discuss them all. I am quite aware that the judgment against Alice Lisle was annulled by Act of Parliament in the following reign. Of the competence and impartiality of that tribunal it is enough to say that only the dogged resistance of the House of Lords prevented the passing of a similar Act to annul the judgment against Titus Oates, and that the House of Commons actually compelled William III. to pardon and pension that unspeakable scoundrel. The one substantial point taken against Jeffreys' conduct of the trial was that he departed from precedent in permitting the Crown to prosecute Alice Lisle for harbouring John Hickes before it had obtained the conviction of Hickes himself. The substantive law having been correctly laid down in the passage which I have quoted, and evidence to prove the fact of Hickes' treason being duly produced, what remained was a question of convenience of procedure. Nor is it easy to see an answer to the point which Jeffreys himself put to the jury: suppose Hickes had been wounded at Sedgemoor and had died in Lady Lisle's house before any question of putting him on his trial could arise, would that have been sufficient to prevent any prosecution for the offence of harbouring the traitor?

The circumstances under which I was impelled to call in aid my recollections of Judge Jeffreys and the opening case of the Bloody Assize, were certainly curious. I had better explain at once that I was not a Judge at the time: I was the Deputy Commissioner of what is called a 'non-regulation' district, an officer who, to the grave reprobation of the politically minded Indian and the advantage of the simple people in his charge, combines with his duties as an executive officer the exercise of very considerable judicial powers. I found myself called upon to deal with one of those epidemics of a particular form of crime which are apt to break out from time to time in an Indian district. Frequently, though not invariably, such an outbreak connotes the presence in the background of a criminal mind of more than usual ability and resource. In this instance the epidemic took the form of blackmail under threat of arson.

In an Indian village the majority of the houses consist of mud walls with thatched roofs; after a spell of dry weather the thatch will burn like tinder. The climate of the Indian plains provides long spells of dry weather, and this is often accompanied by strong winds blowing pretty regularly from a particular direction. A piece of glowing charcoal, or a fragment of dried cow-dung cake smouldering at one end, can be carried about in an earthen pot almost small enough to be concealed in the palm of one hand. The eaves of the humble byres come down low over the ground; it is terribly easy to reach up and thrust the smouldering fire well into the thatch, and the results can be quite amazingly destructive. In a small hamlet every single roof may go up in flames in the course of an hour. The loss and suffering entailed on the little peasant community is not to be measured in money; I know of no meaner form of crime than was the campaign with which I found myself called upon to deal.

It was worked somewhat as follows. Towards the close of the hot season, in one village after another, some mysterious stranger had drifted in. Getting into conversation with the village elders he would bring the talk round to the question of fire, the grave risk of the same in the existing weather conditions and the serious losses which it would cause. One way or another he led up to the announcement that he could guarantee any particular village against fire in return for a small contribution calculated on the size of the place and the paying capacity of the inhabitants. The veiled threat which lurked behind the communication was comprehensible enough, and was thrown into sinister relief by sporadic outbreaks of fire in hamlets which had rejected the proposal with contumely. The setting in of the rainy season brought the operations to an end for the time being. The local police had instituted two or three prosecutions with indifferent success; evidence was desperately hard to obtain. A feeling of insecurity was abroad, and I knew that the possibility of having to add a regular item under the head of 'fire insurance' to the budget of village expenses was being gravely discussed in outlying hamlets in a remote corner of the district.

The rains passed away; the cold weather which followed was even drier than usual. Someone had found the operations of the previous year so profitable that he could hardly wait for the dry March winds to set in before setting his agents to work. The police were on the alert, and the first reports of mysterious fires in that particular neighbourhood were followed by the despatch to the locality of a Sub-Inspector who had a reputation for ferreting out recondite cases of crime. By the time his report came in the situation had become serious. Blackmail was being largely paid, and half a dozen villages within a limited area had been burnt out in the course of three weeks. I was told that the name of the criminal at the bottom of the whole organisation was almost an open secret, but that witnesses were desperately reluctant to speak. Gobardhan was a *brahman* of the highest caste; the trouble was concentrated in an area where the influence of his caste counted for much, and something very like a reign of terror had set in and was intensifying with every week that passed.

I hastily revised my arrangements for the last week of the touring season, sent out my tents, and issued instructions that the arrest should be effected and the witnesses assembled so that I might open the inquiry in the midst of the disturbed area and on the outskirts of a large village about a third of which had been burnt out the week before. On the appointed day I reached my destination after a long morning's march. I had ridden through four villages where the blackened shells of the wretched huts and the sheer misery of the terrified peasants cowering around them, had made their urgent appeal.

The afternoon was well advanced before I could settle down to the hearing of the case, and evidence had to be gone into to prove that the two or three specific cases of arson involved in the charge were part of an organised campaign of blackmail dating back to the year before. Lamps were brought into the tent as I approached the crucial point of the case. In every instance, except one, the blackmail had been demanded through subordinate agents. In the one instance of the village beside which I was encamped, five days before the outbreak of the fire which could be proved by overwhelming circumstantial evidence to have been the work of an incendiary, Gobardhan had come there in person. He had interviewed the village headman, and had taken care that no one else should be within earshot. He had then remained seated in front of the headman's house while the latter went round discussing with one resident after another matters into which the rules of evidence prevented me from inquiring too closely. Eventually, Gobardhan had gone away. The villagers had organised a watch and set patrols to go round the village at night ; but the fire had broken out in the early grey of the morning just five days after Gobardhan's visit. What had the village headman to tell ?

I was sitting at a plain camp table in a large

tent the roof of which was supported upon two tall poles. The prisoner was standing to my right front, the witness almost faced me across the table but a little bit round to my left. The light was supplied by two lamps each lashed to one of the tent-poles, one behind me and one facing me. The lamps were of the kind we used to call 'Hinks's Burners,' without globes but with a metal reflector behind the chimney throwing the light strongly forward. The tent was crowded to suffocation; I had purposely ordered that no villager should be excluded who could find room in which to squat or stand. At an early stage of the headman's examination I found myself straining my eyes for a better view of his face; his words came haltingly, and his eyes were shifting round continually towards the impassive face of the prisoner.

"Surely the light is very bad," I exclaimed.

A head constable came forward. "The lamp behind your Honour's head is going out," he explained, "I think there is not enough oil."

"Take it down and send it out," I ordered. "Tell them to squeeze out the wick and clean the reservoir before refilling it; these wicks clog if the oil is allowed to burn down to the dregs. Meanwhile, take down that other lamp and put it on my table."

As I turned again to the witness the lamp stood just beyond my left elbow; the reflector threw a stream of light across the sheet of foolscap in front of me over which I found it difficult to get a view of his face. Outside the range of the lamp the shadows closed in and a hush of tense expectancy seemed to gather. The examination continued somewhat as follows :—

" The accused, Gobardhan *brahman*, sat down with you on the raised platform just outside your door ; what did he say ? "

" He said—I cannot remember everything he said. I am an old man and I have been ruined by this fire ; how can I remember exactly what the accused said to me ? "

" You may be able to remember a little at a time. What was the subject of his conversation ? "

" He talked—we talked—about fire, about the fires at Bari Nagla and Bhainsgaon."

" How far is Bari Nagla from your village ? "

" Four miles away to the east, your Honour."

" And Bhainsgaon ? "

" A little farther off, and more to the north."

" Well—what did the accused say about the fires in those two places ? "

" He said—he said—he was very sorry for the men of Bhainsgaon and Bari Nagla."

" What else ? "

" He was very sorry for them. I am a poor man and very old, and all my household goods have been burnt. How can I remember things ? "

Yes—it was I who was beginning to ' remember things.' It all came over me, the darkened court, the stammering reluctant witness, the grim voice ordering that a candle be held to him to show up his impudent brazen face. There might be something in it; one could but try, anyhow. I raised my voice just a little that there might be no mistake about its being clearly audible to the villagers crowding the dark corners of the tent. I spoke slowly, choosing my words.

"I begin to think that this witness is trying not to speak the truth. It is a dangerous thing to give false evidence, and a man ought to be ashamed to tell lies in the presence of all his caste-fellows and neighbours. Also, no man should be afraid to speak the truth in the presence of the *Sirkar*." I purposely gave myself the title of honour which to the Indian villager connotes the mysterious Government under which he lives. I turned to the head constable. "I want to see the face of the witness clearly so that I can tell if he is not speaking the truth. Turn the lamp round towards him. No—that will not do. Bring my office-box forward and stand the lamp on it, now turn it round. Never mind my paper, I can see well enough to write down the truth if I hear it. I want to see the face of the witness. Yes, that will do."

The man blinked painfully as the reflector concentrated the light on his face.

"There is nothing to fear," I said. "The light will not hurt your eyes if you speak the truth. I am only going to ask you one or two quite simple questions; you are not too old or too poor to give me a plain answer. Now, the accused was very sorry for the men of Bhainsgaon and Bari Nagla; did he say why he was sorry?"

His eyes turned downwards, but his face was in a blaze of light and he dared not look round towards the prisoner. The words came in jerks. "He said—he said they had been very obstinate. They had lost much more money in consequence of the fire than they would have had to pay to prevent it."

"Gobardhan said that?"

"Yes, your Honour. How should I know about it if he had not said it?"

I was conscious of a quickening pulse, but I controlled my voice.

"I suppose your village would have had to pay more?"

"Much more. He said we were a larger village and had more money."

"Was any sum mentioned?"

The eyes lifted, staring hypnotically at the glare of the lamp; the tongue wavered over the parched lips. Then the words came with a rush.

"He wanted too much—far too much. He said the contribution for my village was fifty rupees, but he would take forty rupees if I would collect the money at once. Your Honour, where were we to find forty rupees? The others said I had more than that buried in my house: it is a lie, you can search my house, you can dig up all the floor. They said they would give ten rupees if I gave the rest; where was I to find thirty rupees?"

"It was most unfair," I said calmly. "You can wait now while I write that down." I reached forward and turned the lamp round. It had served its purpose, the ice was broken now. I not only secured a clear and convincing statement from the headman, but corroboration was forthcoming as to what passed between his failure to raise the forty rupees and the departure of the accused, with ominous words which others besides the headman had heard. Before the court rose, adjourning the case to allow the accused time to prepare his defence and every other privilege he could claim under the Criminal Procedure Code, I had an unbreakable case against him on the record before me.

I have always thought that a stronger hand than mine was raised against Gobardhan *brahman*: he died in prison before he had served the first year of the sentence I passed upon him.

II.

A CLASH OF SUPERSTITIONS.

I suppose it is permissible to raise the question why the great architect of the universe has not seen fit so to arrange the movements of the planet earth, in relation to the two heavenly bodies which most concern it, as to make the computation of the phenomenon we call 'time' a less complicated matter to our limited intelligences. We start, as one of the most ancient of our records has it, by noting that "there was evening and there was morning, one day." We pass on to consider the regularly recurrent changes in the 'lesser light' which we conceive Him to have set "to rule the night," and so arrive at the notion of a period of time which we call a 'month.' Finally, the process of the seasons gives us the concept of the 'year.'

This we now understand to represent one revolution of our planet round the 'greater light' which we call the sun. One wonders when and how mankind first realised the inconveniences resulting from the fact that neither the 'solar year' nor the 'lunar month' is to be measured in a complete number of 'days,' and the further fact that the former is anything but an exact multiple of the latter. When we were very young we were told—at least I know I was—that the moon revolved round the earth in twenty-eight days. For practical purposes it does nothing of the sort; and personally it was only after I had arrived in India, and was trying to understand Hindu and Mohammedan calendars, that I had the curiosity to inquire into the varying lengths of our own months and the fallacy lurking behind the statement that "twelve months make one year."

Of course, the fact is that the movement of the moon round the earth is complicated by the revolution of the earth round its own axis, so that a 'lunation,' the interval between full moon and full moon (or, for the matter of that, between new moon and new moon) at any given spot on the earth's surface represents a period of 29 days, 12 hours, 44 minutes, and 2.8 seconds. I will not undertake to explain why, but that fraction of a second is a great joy to me. The 'solar year' is computed to consist of 365 days, 5 hours, 48 minutes, and 46 seconds. Hence mankind has had to face a double problem. The calendar year must consist of an entire number of days, and a number of expedients were tried and arbitrary conventions enforced before Western civilisation arrived at the complicated arrangement of 'leap years' which keeps our calendar year in practical correspondence with the process of the seasons, as determined by the annual motion of the earth. Even now astronomers tell us that, if we reach the year 4000 A.D., it will be advisable to enact that this shall be a common year and not a leap year, as it would be under the ordinary rule. The other problem, that of maintaining some correspondence between the 'calendar month' and the actual movements of the earth's satellite, we Westerners have given up as insoluble. Our 'months' are artificial divisions of time, and we must refer to a printed calendar to ascertain on what days in any given month the phenomena of 'new moon' and 'full moon' may be expected to occur.

In India the problem is conditioned by the needs of a more primitive civilisation and the requirements of religious systems deeply interwoven with the daily life of the people. To Hindus and Mohammedans alike the phases of the moon dictate the appropriate days for solemn festivals and religious observances of various kinds; for them it is more important that the calendar should conform to the lunar months than that it should take strict account of the process of the seasons involved in the solar year. We should think it intolerable that the 1st of January should wander backwards through the seasons and turn up, it may be, on Midsummer Day; to the Mohammedan it is far more unthinkable that the first day of the month should be other than the day of the new moon. I suppose the social conditions of Arabia in the time of the Prophet Mohammed, and the comparatively monotonous climate of that country, are responsible for the fact that the Mohammedan calendar ignores the 'solar year' as completely as Western civilisation has elected to ignore the 'lunar month.' The Mohammedan year consists of twelve 'lunations'; it is kept in substantial harmony with the phases of the moon by reckoning nineteen years out of every thirty as 354 days, and the remaining eleven as years of 355 days. Each month is supposed to begin with the new moon; every now and then a doubt whether the new moon will be actually visible in the brief interval available after sunset on a particular day compels a long-suffering Government to arrange alternative dates for an important Mohammedan festival. Indeed, I can remember one year in which the two rival sects of Islam—the *Sunnis* and the *Shias*—differed as to whether the moon had or had not been visible on a certain evening, and insisted on observing the Festival of Sacrifice on two consecutive days; in an important town of Oudh this insistence provoked the Hindus to a sanguinary riot. Other inconveniences attach to the observance of a calendar which goes drifting backwards through the solar year, completing the circuit of the seasons once in every 32½ years or thereabouts. One is that devout followers of Islam find themselves keeping the grim fast of the month of Ramazan, during which neither food nor water may pass their lips between sunrise and sunset, in the midst of the torrid summer heat of the Indian plains.

The Hindus are more fortunate, in that they employ a calendar evolved in their own country and adapted to its needs. The precise times of the great religious festivals are still determined by the phases of the moon, so that the year is necessarily composed of lunar months. They understand both ways of reckoning the month—that is, from new moon to new moon and from full moon to full moon; but in Northern India at any rate the full moon may be regarded as marking the last day of a month. At the same time, a people mainly dependent upon agriculture, and living in a country of marked and regular climatic variations, could not tolerate a calendar year wholly dissociated from the progress of the seasons. The difficulty is met by the use of intercalary months. The details of the system are complicated and depend upon the estimated times of the sun's entry into the different signs of the zodiac; but for practical purposes it may be said that, after the lunar year of the Hindus has worked back for twenty days or so along the solar year, it will be thrust forward again in the course of the following twelvemonth by reckoning some one month twice over, as, for instance, by having a 'first *Asarh*' and a 'second *Asarh*' before proceeding to the next month of *Sawan*.

This is why, in a previous chapter, I was able to speak of the Bathing Festival celebrated on the last day of the month of *Kartik* as held upon the full moon of November. A greater and more popular festival of the Hindus may similarly be referred to as connected with the full moon of March. The name of this festival has a curious sound to English ears, for it is called the *Holi*. It is essentially the festival of the spring Equinox; it presents features which seem to carry it far back in the history of mankind and to connect it with the primitive folklore of other peoples. To the lower orders it means four or five days of license and revelry, reminiscent of the Saturnalia of the Romans; and there is a tradition of trying to send people off upon bootless errands which reminds one of 'April Fool's Day.' The story I am leading up to, however, is concerned with another of the observances of the day, the bonfire which it is customary to kindle on the night of the full moon. Whatever may be the religious significance of this rite, certain curious superstitions have grown up in connection with it in rural India. If a torch is kindled at this bonfire, and extinguished before it has burnt itself out, the blackened stump is known as a 'murda'—that is to say, 'a corpse.' Now a corpse is an unlucky thing to come across or to handle; if you can introduce a corpse into your enemy's house, or even lay it at his door, you may congratulate yourself on having called down misfortune upon his head. A tradition seems to have grown up that the extinguished torches from the sacred bonfire will have the same effect as a real corpse.

A more definitely rustic belief is that linseed, gathered by the light of the full moon of March, and dried in the smoke of the sacred bonfire, will serve as a charm to keep bugs out of bedsteads. Very early in my Indian service I came upon a case in which the accidental clashing of these two superstitions led to a tragedy; the circumstances were impressed on my mind by a feeling of remorse for having precipitated the ultimate climax by ill-considered conduct of my own.

The reader must picture to himself three hamlets —we may call them Lalganj, Rasra, and Bansdih —so situated that the village sites form a rough triangle and the boundaries of the village lands converge at a particular point. Of the three, Lalganj was the largest and most important. The landholders belonged to one of the old Hindu fighting clans, and, in fact, relatives of theirs were serving in the infantry regiment stationed at Benares. They were, as the event proved, of a pugnacious disposition; and in this very month of March they had started a very pretty quarrel with the residents of Rasra over some cattle which had trespassed across the village boundary and had been forcibly rescued by the Lalganj men as the owners of the damaged fields in Rasra attempted to take them to the pound. The quarrel was suspended during the *Holi* festivities, and the night of the full moon saw the sacred bonfires kindled in each of the three villages and the customary festivities in full swing.

The story now shifts to the hamlet of Bansdih, which had no concern whatever with the feud maturing between its two neighbours. One or two careful housewives of this place had bethought them of the benefits to be obtained from linseed gathered on this particular night, and sent out five or six boys—the oldest was about fourteen—to go and collect some. It so happened that this could most conveniently be done in certain fields situated at about the point where the village boundary converged towards the boundaries of Rasra and Lalganj ; the lie of the ground was such that it sloped downwards in that direction from each of the village sites, the rise being most marked towards the houses of Lalganj. There was no particular reason why the boys should not have been content to carry out their task by the light of the full moon ; but the fatality which brooded over the events of that night decreed that they should take with them three or four torches, possibly as an extra precaution against the risk of damaging other crops in the quest for linseed, or it may be merely as part of a game they were making out of the occasion. To complete the setting for the impending tragedy, it further happened that someone or other amongst the merrymakers round the bonfire at Bansdih remembered that there were early-reaped crops lying in their threshing-floor, on the opposite side of the village site from that on which the bonfire had been kindled, and suggested that it might be prudent to have a man on guard there. Thereupon Mangal, *brahman*, an elderly man who had seen many *Holi* bonfires in his time, and was quite ready to oblige the younger folk, volunteered to act as watchman for the night. Stepping into his own courtyard to collect his quarterstaff of stout bamboo, he walked over to the threshing-floor and sat down; the boys ran past him, laughing and joking, on their way to the fields where they were to look for linseed.

Thus it came about that some resident of Lalganj, glancing downwards across the village lands, noticed the smoky light of torches flickering among the fields where his boundary converged towards those of Rasra and Bansdih. He called to some of his neighbours and pointed in that direction. I fancy the Lalganj men were not quite easy in their minds about their own high-handed conduct in the matter of the trespassing cattle; at any rate they were quick to jump to conclusions.

"See there, brothers," cried one, "this is the infamous conduct of those scoundrels at Rasra. Not content with filing a petition in court against us, stuffed full of falsehoods, about the cattle they tried to impound, they are now trying to bring ill-fortune upon us during the coming year. Those torches must have been kindled at their *Holi* fire; presently they will extinguish them and throw the *murdas* over the boundary on to our lands. Is this sort of thing to be endured?"

The general feeling was that it was not, that the time had come to teach the men of Rasra a lesson. A party of nine of the Lalganj landholders armed themselves and set out down the slope. Seven of them carried only the *lathi*, the bamboo quarterstaff; but two men most unhappily contrived to snatch up more efficient weapons. Jaipal Rae carried an axe; while Shankar Rae picked up a long iron shaft, such as is used locally to stir the furnace under the vats in which the sap of the sugar-cane is boiled. This particular implement had been sharpened to a point at one end, making it into a very efficient spear.

One may imagine the amazement and alarm of the little fellows from Bansdih, all unconscious of evil intent and making a merry jest of the errand on which their mothers had sent them, as they found a group of angry men bearing down upon them, shouting out threats and abuse. They stopped for no explanations; dropping everything they carried, they ran hard for the shelter of their own village. By this time the party from Lalganj must have fully realised that their wrath was groundless, and that they had set out under a misapprehension; but it is always easier to lose your temper than to recover your self-control. Someone called out that the little beggars deserved a hiding anyhow, if only for the fright they had given and the trouble they had caused. There may have been a moment of hesitation, but presently the Lalganj men came running towards Bansdih after the frightened boys. Mangal had risen to his feet as he heard the cries and the uproar of voices in anger. He was standing on the edge of the threshing-floor, quarterstaff in hand, as the boys rushed past him, crying for help; the party from Lalganj came hard on their heels. There was a moment or two of confused parleying. The Lalganj men shouted that they meant to give the boys a hiding. Mangal replied that the boys had done nothing wrong, and that no one should lay a finger on them while he was there to prevent it.

Jaipal Rae and Shankar Rae had thrust their way to the front. One of the controverted points at the subsequent trial was whether there had not been a definite interval of space between them and the rest of their party; another was whether they were not spurred to action by cries of "Strike! Strike!" from the men behind them. At any rate, Jaipal Rae ended the parley by stepping forward and striking with his axe at the old man's head. As Mangal caught the blow on his trusty quarterstaff, Shankar Rae lunged out with his improvised spear; the point took Mangal full in the throat. The two assailants stepped back, whether aghast at their own work, or prepared to strike again if necessary, God alone knows. The old *brahman* dropped his weapon, turned, staggered three or four paces in the direction of his house, and fell dead. The men from Lalganj turned and ran for their own village.

What followed may serve to illustrate some of the difficulties and complications attendant on the administration of the criminal law in India. When the investigating police officer reached Lalganj there was no adult male of military age to be found amongst the landholders of the village. This was quite in accordance with what that officer must have expected from previous experience of crimes committed in the course of a village riot or affray. The guilty parties abscond because their absence makes it more difficult to collect evidence implicating them personally in the affair, and because there is always the chance of preparing a really serviceable *alibi*. Their innocent caste-fellows will abscond, partly in order to avoid having to answer inconvenient questions, and also because the more of them are found absent on the day after the crime, the less cogent does the mere fact of such absence become as a piece of evidence against any one of the guilty persons. In this instance the first arrests were effected in consequence of inquiries discreetly made at and about native infantry barracks at Benares, where the Lalganj men had relatives amongst the sepoys; moreover, Shankar Rae produced really impressive evidence to prove that he had spent the entire *Holi* festival with a brother-in-law at Benares.

I have anticipated matters a little, because the investigating sub-inspector had to make out a list of the party which had sallied out from Lalganj before he could set about arresting any of them. Two or three of the boys who had gone to gather linseed were of an age to make their evidence important. They knew the landholders of Lalganj well enough by sight, and their story of the actual killing of Mangal by Shankar Rae and Jaipal Rae was corroborated by one or two men of their village who had hurried towards the threshing-floor at the first sound of the altercation. It was extremely doubtful, however, if these men had seen enough of the rest of the party from Lalganj to be able to recognise any of them with certainty; and the same remark applied, to a lesser extent, to the testimony of the little boys.

There was, moreover, one question going to the root of the whole case, the difficulty of which was either overlooked or deliberately ignored by the worthy sub-inspector. The killing of Mangal *brahman* by the two men who actually struck at him was sheer murder; I have never been able to understand how anyone, with the Indian Penal Code in front of him, can have regarded it as anything less. The old man had offered no provocation beyond endeavouring to prevent the Lalganj men from thrashing the unfortunate boys, a thing they had obviously no right to do. It is true there is a certain clause in the Code which reduces the guilt of homicide, in certain cases, where death has been caused without premeditation in a fair fight; but there was no semblance of 'fair fighting' about this onslaught of two strapping youths, each better armed than himself, upon one old man. To the Sub-Inspector, however, the matter seems to have been hopelessly complicated by the further question of the degree of criminality attaching to the conduct of the other men who had accompanied Shankar Rae and Jaipal Rae from Lalganj. Within the meaning of a certain definition in the Indian Penal Code the whole party constituted a "wrongful assembly," when it set out with the intention of waging a private feud against presumed offenders from Rasra. Their assembly became, if I may so put it, even more obviously 'wrongful' when they elected to pursue the unfortunate little boys from Bansdih who had done nothing which they were in the slightest degree entitled to resent. Now, under the Indian Penal Code every person who intentionally joins an 'unlawful assembly' becomes liable for acts of violence done by a member of that 'assembly' in pursuance of the 'common object' of the same. It may fairly be assumed that the 'common object' of the Lalganj men, by the time they reached the threshing-floor at Bansdih, was to inflict a thrashing on the little boys who had, quite innocently, excited their alarm by carrying torches when they went to gather linseed. Was the killing of Mangal an act done in the prosecution of that 'common object'? Or was that killing itself to be treated as having become a 'common object' of the assembly, because there was evidence that Mangal's remonstrances had been received with cries of "Strike! Strike!" proceeding from the group immediately behind the two leaders?

It has been my experience more than once that the entire course of a criminal investigation may be turned in a wrong direction by reason of the fact that it is entered upon under the influence of some misconception; also that it is desperately hard to get the thing back on to the right line if it once starts on a wrong tack. In the present case the Sub-Inspector had set out with the notion that he had to deal with a 'riot,' a death caused in the course of an affray in which a number of men had acted in concert. The obvious difficulty of holding every member of the Lalganj party guilty of stark murder obscured to his mind the plain fact that a murder had been committed. He was also obsessed with the belief that he would be held to have failed in his duty unless he could collect evidence sufficient to convict all the men who had set out from Lalganj of some offence or other. By treating the killing of Mangal as an act of "culpable homicide not amounting to murder"—what we should call 'manslaughter' in England,—he actually secured a little (somewhat dubious) evidence from Lalganj itself to help him to fix the identity of some of the 'rioters.'

The investigating police officer having started the case on the wrong line, it became the duty of the committing magistrate to try and straighten it out. Whatever the precise reason may have been, and I could suggest several, that officer treated the case in routine fashion just as it was laid before him by the police. In the first instance Shankar Rae and three members of the little company which had stood at his back while he and Jaipal Rae struck the old man down, were put on their trial for "culpable homicide not amounting to murder." The course of the trial was such as to thrust into prominence the question of the value of Shankar Rae's *alibi*, and the identification evidence against the other three. The Sessions

Judge dealt with the case on the footing on which it was presented to him: he acquitted one of the accused on the insufficiency of his identification, and convicted Shankar Rae and the other two on the charge as framed. He sentenced Shankar Rae to rigorous imprisonment (the equivalent of penal servitude) for eight years, and passed lesser sentences on the other two. Their appeals came before the High Court and were dismissed, the learned Judge who heard them dealing mainly with Shankar Rae's *alibi* and the identification evidence, and accepting the statements of two of the little boys to the effect that the others had called upon Shankar Rae and Jaipal Rae to strike. I may add that while the High Court possesses very large powers of superintendence over the proceedings of all courts subordinate to it, the question whether the killing of Mangal had not been an act of murder pure and simple could not very well have been raised except upon an appeal by the Local Government, or by the cumbrous procedure incident upon the ordering of a new trial.

Later on, two more of the Lalganj men were arrested, sent up for trial, and acquitted by the Sessions Judge on the weakness of the identification evidence. Unhappily for himself, as the event proved, Jaipal Rae succeeded in evading arrest for eight or nine months. By that time one of the numerous transfers to which one is liable in the early part of one's service had sent me to the district, and I was the committing magistrate before whom the police produced Jaipal Rae and two other men of the party whom they had arrested along with him, or at about the same time. It so happened, also, that the case came to me during my cold weather tour. I was in camp near Lalganj. I visited the village and saw Mangal's widow and children while the proceedings in my court were pending. The man must have married—or more probably remarried—somewhat late in life, for the children I saw were quite young.

Now, it was undoubtedly my duty to deal with the case on the evidence before me and on the facts disclosed by that evidence, independently of any proceedings previously had against other persons accused in the same matter. I found the identification evidence against two of my accused decidedly weak, and I accepted the responsibility of discharging them. As for the killing of Mangal, I could not, in honour and conscience, treat it as anything but an act of murder. Nor could I see any difference in guilt, legal or moral, between Shankar Rae and Jaipal Rae. Both had struck at the old man with lethal weapons blows of deadly import; it was a mere accident of the affray that the axe had been warded off while the spear had struck home. Moreover, if the victim's weapon had not been occupied in guarding his head from Jaipal Rae's axe, it would have been available to parry Shankar Rae's spear. I have never doubted that I did my plain duty in committing Jaipal Rae to stand his trial on a charge of murder.

What the result would have been if his case had come before the courts of superior jurisdiction I hardly know. It is at least possible that the said courts might have found valid reasons for adhering to the view of the law applicable to the facts of the case which they had previously, by implication, laid down. I might have got nothing for my trouble but a snub for professing to know so much more about the law of homicide than my elders and betters. That would not have troubled me greatly; what my conscience has to answer is that I went beyond the requirements of duty in this case and brought about a result which I certainly never contemplated.

I would have the reader remember that I was young and inexperienced; also, that my feelings had been stirred by the sight of the widow and children of the courageous and inoffensive old man who had, in my opinion, been foully murdered. I gave way to a surge of anger against the wretched prisoner before me. It was right that I should explain to him the precise meaning of the order I was passing on his case, but I did so in vindictive fashion, seeking to inspire terror and awaken remorse. I told him that the killing of Mangal was in my opinion a murder pure and simple, a case for the hangman's rope. I explained precisely why I could see no difference between his guilt and that of Shankar Rae; adding that they, both of them, had the death of a *brahman* on their souls, which I understood their religion regarded as a terrible thing. I went on to say that, unfortunately in my opinion, there was no chance of his being hanged, as Shankar Rae had got off with a sentence of eight years' imprisonment; but that the law allowed an alternative sentence of transportation for life in cases of murder, that I was doing my level best to ensure his receiving that sentence, which was the least that could be passed upon him if he were found guilty on the charge I had framed.

Apart altogether from the fact that it was no business of mine to browbeat the wretched man in this fashion, there are two points about this oration which I particularly regret. I had no real expectation of getting the man punished with transportation for life: even in the improbable event of my so framing the proceedings in my court as to coerce the courts above me into recording a conviction of murder, it was sufficiently clear to me that means would be found, if only by invoking the clemency of the Crown, to ensure that his punishment should at least not exceed that of Shankar Rae. In the second place, the fact that Mangal was a *brahman* meant nothing to me; I should have felt just the same about the matter if he had belonged to a lower caste. I was, therefore, brandishing over the head of the unhappy man supernatural terrors in which I did not believe, and the threat of a temporal penalty which I was practically certain that he would never incur.

In estimating the consequences of my rashly spoken words, something must be said about the sentence of transportation for life. I do not quite know what this sentence involves nowadays; at the time of which I write it meant a transfer to the Penal Settlement in the Andaman Islands. There, after a short period of rigid discipline, a well-conducted convict might hope to receive various relaxations, culminating in his release at the end of twenty years and his return to his own country. If, however, it be a desirable thing that a punishment should be deterrent out of all proportion to its real severity, then this sentence of transportation for life was an ideal weapon in the legislative armoury. To a villager of Jaipal Rae's caste it meant a journey across the dreaded and defiling 'black water' into a life of unknown hardships; and I have no doubt the wretched man thought that the fatal words 'for life' meant precisely what they said.

I shall never know exactly where my words had struck home, but this is what followed. Jaipal Rae was taken from my camp to the district jail, and that night he was confined in a solitary cell. Above his head, but well within reach of his arm, was a barred window. He was wearing, whether as turban or as loincloth I am not sure, a long and narrow piece of cloth, thin enough to be rolled or twisted into a convenient rope. Having so arranged the cloth he tied one end of it firmly to the window bars. Allowing the full length of the cloth in between, he looped the other end about his own neck, took a firm hold on each side of the noose and pulled hard. As unconsciousness overcame him he fell forward the length of his improvised rope. He was found in the morning, half-strangled, half-hanged, and quite dead.

The essential fault which I find in my dealings with this man is that, going beyond the duties of my office, I had taken it upon myself to sit in judgment upon a fellow-creature in a fashion which appertains only to the God who made us all. Some primeval instinct within me had cried out that the murder of the old *brahman* demanded punishment on the ancient scale of a life for a life. I had said openly that I only wished it were in my power to enforce that punishment. The granting of my wish came to me as a rebuke and a warning.

> " God answers sharp and sudden on some prayers,
> And flings the thing we asked for in our face,
> A gauntlet, with a gift in it."

III.

A MOHARRAM RIOT.

CHAPTER I.

SUNNIS AND SHIAS.

To one who has studied the history which lies behind it, there is something anomalous about the celebration in India of the great Mohammedan festival of the *Moharram*. Looked at from one point of view, the thing is almost as great a paradox as it would be to find a Christian community, the overwhelming majority of which adhered to the Roman Catholic faith, enthusiastically adopting a day originally set apart by the Protestant minority for the commemoration of the martyrs, Latimer and Ridley, who perished at the stake in defence of their peculiar doctrines, and treating it as a memorial and proclamation of the steadfastness and heroism which Christians of old displayed under distressing circumstances. I do not say that the parallel is an exact one, but it may serve to suggest to English readers something of the true position and help them to understand the difficulties which may from time to time confront those responsible for seeing that the celebrations are duly carried out year by year. It has been one of the accidents of my Indian career to have had a great deal to do with this matter at different times and in various ways. I propose to see how much of the interest it has always excited in my mind I can contrive to communicate to others.

I still remember with amusement my first actual contact with a Moharram procession. I was at the time an Assistant Magistrate of less than two years' service, and no one would have thought of leaving me in charge of the Moharram arrangements in an important town like Mirzapur. The responsibility was thrust upon me by the fact that two English officers, older and more experienced than myself, went down with fever on the very day of the celebration. The procession was to pass down the main street of the city after dark, and I rode to the central police station at the appointed hour with my nerves a great deal more on edge than they had any call to be. I knew in a general way that the Moharram was a festival in honour of Hassan and Husain, grandsons of the founder of Islam by his daughter, Fatima; that it was supposed in some way to arouse Moslem fanaticism to a high pitch and that all sorts of terrible things might happen if that fanaticism were provoked by any interference, real or imaginary, with the celebrations on the part of the Hindus. The head of the procession was just approaching the police station when, from somewhere farther up its course, came the sound of a loud explosion followed by shrieks and cries of pain. In a moment I was on the back of my pony, police officers and constables helping me to push my way through the throng towards the scene of the alarm. I had nothing worse to deal with than a quite excusable panic caused by the rashness of an individual who had seen fit to join a procession in which flaring torches were being carried, having upon his back a large bundle of fireworks.

Later on I was to learn a great deal more about the Moharram, and this in particular—that the risk of its provoking disturbances between Mohammedan and Hindu is of less importance than the animosity it is capable of arousing between the rival sects of Islam, the *Sunnis* and the *Shias*. The danger is inherent at once in the history of the great schism of Islam, and in the nature of the historical event which the procession held on the tenth day of the Mohammedan month of Moharram is supposed to commemorate.

From one point of view it may be said that the schism arises out of a dispute concerning the succession to the spiritual and temporal Headship of Islam which broke out immediately upon the death of its Founder, but it is truer and more enlightening to regard it as one of the consequences of the Moslem conquest of Persia. To me it has never been matter for surprise that learned and devout Moslems should refer to the amazing conquests effected by their armies during the ten years that followed the death of the Prophet, as evidence of the divine origin of their faith. The story is an astounding one. Mohammed died in 632 A.D. Some three years before his death he was fighting desperately with his back to the wall to maintain his recent conquest of the holy city of Mecca against a coalition of Arab tribes. Nothing but his own invincible resolution and the heroism of his son-in-law, Ali, won him the victory in a battle which had been within an ace of proving an irreparable disaster. Within three years of his death Moslem armies had entered Damascus as conquerors. A year later the Emperor of Constantinople was beaten in a great battle which finally made over Syria to Arab rule. Simultaneously campaigns were being conducted against the Persians for the possession of Mesopotamia. The victory of Kadisiya, which gave what we now call Iraq to the Moslems, came in 637 A.D. Three years later Egypt was added to the Moslem Empire. This was now a fairly compact and manageable concern, extending mainly over lands Semitic rather than Aryan by race, portions of which had been the scene of Arab immigration in the past. The subject populations had been long under alien rule; to the majority of Oriental Christians it came as a positive relief to pass under the sway of rulers who at any rate knew no distinction between one particular brand of Christianity and another. It needed only the steady pressure of the civil disabilities imposed upon non-Moslems to win over the masses to the faith of their conquerors. It was an empire over which an Arab

Caliph, with his temporal capital at Medina or at Damascus, and his spiritual capital at Mecca, might long have maintained the supremacy of his race.

It is true that upon all its frontiers a Moslem Empire stood committed to a policy of expansion, and that this tended inevitably to shift its centre of gravity away from Arabia. Constant warfare with the Byzantine Empire made Damascus a more important capital than Medina, but the real trouble was on the side of Persia. There the Arabs encountered a national feeling stronger than their own, and a religion which was still a living force. The Persians felt towards the Arabs a mixture of fear and contempt, the latter resting on a belief in the superiority of their own civilisation, the former on a subconscious sense of the superior fighting qualities of the men of the deserts. Apart altogether from the outward thrust of Islam, the Persians themselves could not submit to see their empire stripped of its fairest provinces. They continued the struggle until they were utterly broken. The decisive battle came in 641 A.D., and the Moslem tide submerged Persia proper. The struggle was a bitter one, and even when the conquered—those of them who did not prefer a voluntary exile—accepted the religion of their conquerors, they brought into it a leaven of foreign ideas. Amongst these were the concept of hereditary monarchy and that of semi-divine attributes surrounding the person of the monarch, both alien to the essential democracy of Arabia.

Anything in the nature of a dynastic quarrel amongst the Arabs themselves would offer the newly converted Moslems of Persia the opportunity for adopting a policy of their own in opposition to that of their Arab masters.

On the death of the Prophet Mohammed the duty of choosing, or at least of accepting, some one person to be his 'representative,' the religious head of the new faith and the ruler who should maintain the union of the Arab tribes, necessarily fell to the assembly of his leading adherents and supporters which came together at Medina. The choice fell in the first instance upon Abu Bakr, the friend and father-in-law of the Prophet. He died after a short reign, the principal work of which was to suppress an attempt on the part of various Arab tribes to break away from the supremacy of Medina and Mecca, if not from the essential tenets of Islam itself. At the time of his death it was absolutely necessary that a successor should be found whose position commanded respect, and who possessed the gifts of leadership required to control and direct the impending outward thrust of Islam into the countries bordering Arabia. Such a man was found in the Caliph Omar, who had also given a daughter in marriage to the Prophet. His reign of ten years was the era of the great conquests; but while his armies were spreading the domination of Arabia and the faith of Islam over Syria, Mesopotamia, and Egypt, he failed to protect his own life from the vengeance of the subject populations. A common workman from the town of Kufa in Iraq stabbed the great conqueror in the mosque at Medina. Omar had been statesman enough to foresee the necessity of making provision for the succession, but he did so in a peculiar fashion. He named six men of the great chiefs and leaders of Islam, with directions that they should assemble upon his death and choose a Caliph from amongst their own number. The natural result was that the choice fell upon a man already advanced in years, and not the strongest personality amongst the candidates. The name of the third Caliph appears in most histories as Othman ; the Indian Moslems call him Usman. He ruled for twelve troubled years, during which the substance of power was passing more and more into the hands of the Meccan aristocracy, and agitation against the Caliph and his governors was growing, especially in Egypt and in Iraq. At Damascus Usman's cousin, Moawiya, was ruling with a firm hand in the Caliph's name. Gradually the name of Ali came more and more into prominence as the head, or at least the figurehead, of an agitation which was, in part at any rate, a Puritan movement of protest against the growing worldliness and dissoluteness of manners beginning to manifest themselves in a class enriched by the spoils of the great conquests. Ali had married the favourite daughter of Mohammed ; he was himself a cousin of the Prophet, and his sons were in lineal descent from the Founder of Islam. He had been the fighting hero of the great battle which had finally brought the whole of Arabia under the Prophet's rule. Already men were whispering to one another that Mohammed had in fact designated Ali as his successor, that the Caliphates of Abu Bakr, Omar, and Usman, if not actual usurpations, could only be regarded as temporary arrangements acquiesced in by Ali while he still felt himself too young to assume the burden of the sovereignty. The paradox of the situation was that, while armies which owed allegiance to Usman were pressing on Islam's career of conquest in Africa, in Asia Minor, in Central Asia, and across the frontiers of India, the aged Caliph found himself helpless in his house at Medina confronted by deputations of his own subjects who had come from Egypt and from Iraq, with arms in their hands, to represent their grievances and clamour for redress. There was some confused bargaining, a sudden outcry that the Caliph was tricking them with promises never intended to be kept, and the old man of eighty was done to death by a handful of furious malcontents.

The verdict of history acquits Ali of complicity in the murder, just as it must acquit Moawiya of the meaner charge that he had deliberately refrained, out of selfish policy, from sending help to his overlord at the critical moment; but it remained a reproach against Ali that he did nothing to punish the murderers. It was the mutineers, some of whom at any rate were responsible for that murder, who acclaimed him as Caliph, and it was the support of the party which had risen against Usman that enabled him to tread down opposition and establish himself as sovereign in Arabia and in Iraq. In Damascus he was never acknowledged. Moawiya held Syria against him and finally claimed the Caliphate for himself. There was some fighting and an attempt at arbitration. Ali's strength was in Iraq, where his partisans mustered in the great towns of Kufa and Basra, and the movement that was to take shape later in the formation of the Shia sect was working in his favour. The essential difficulty of his position was that he had been placed at the head of a coalition of malcontents, representing hopelessly divergent ideals and interests. Much of his time and energy were dissipated in enforcing obedience upon one section or another of his nominal adherents. His cause was steadily losing ground when he himself fell by the hand of an assassin, the third Caliph in succession to perish by violence in a period of seventeen years.

The immediate result of Ali's death was to establish the authority of Moawiya as Caliph over all the territories of Islam. In Mesopotamia the partisans of Ali made an attempt to set up his eldest son, Hassan, but the movement collapsed without fighting. Hassan made terms for himself in a fashion which excited a mutiny amongst his own followers; he withdrew to Medina and lived there in retirement until his death eight or nine years later. Moawiya proved himself an able and energetic ruler; he succeeded in founding, in his own family of the Omayyads, a dynasty which ruled over Islam from Damascus for close upon ninety years. His own reign covered the first nineteen years of this period and he was able to secure the succession for his son, Yazid.

As soon as it was known in Mesopotamia that Moawiya was dead and that Yazid had been proclaimed Caliph at Damascus, the partisans of Ali stirred once again. A message was sent from influential chiefs at Kufa to Husain, the second son of Ali, then living quietly at Mecca, inviting him to Iraq and promising to acknowledge him as Caliph on his appearing amongst them. On the eighth day of the month preceding the Moharram, Husain set out from Mecca at the head of a considerable force, but one hopelessly inadequate for his purpose unless its appearance in Iraq should provoke a general rising in his favour. At Karbala, west of the Euphrates, he was intercepted by superior forces supporting the Caliph of Damascus. No help reached him from Kufa and he was left to fight out the issue at the head of the devoted adherents who had accompanied him from Arabia. The battle was fought on the tenth day of the month of Moharram; it ended in the death of Husain and the practical annihilation of his small army.

Nevertheless, it was upon the assassination of Ali and the disaster of Karbala that the party now known as the *Shias* (the word in itself means simply a 'party' or 'sect') consolidated itself and gathered strength. The death of Ali covered with the halo of martyrdom his virtual failure as a ruler, and no devout Moslem could ponder without feelings of compunction and regret, which an adroit propaganda might easily stir into fierce indignation, on the fact that a grandson of the Prophet had fallen in battle by Moslem hands. The strength of the Shias lay amongst the newly-converted Moslems of Persia and the system they developed was tinged with Persian ideas. They taught that the Headship of Islam was not an office which could be conferred by human election ; it was given of God and hereditary in the family of the Prophet. The superhuman powers of Mohammed descended as an inheritance in his house, so that from Ali came a line of *Imams* to whom, and not to the ruling Caliph for the time being, the allegiance of the faithful was rightly due. The discontent and resentment against Arab domination, widely prevalent amongst the new Moslems in the eastern part of the Empire, was fostered by a persistent campaign of slander and vilification directed against the Omayyad dynasty. It became almost an article of faith that Moawiya had caused the death of Hassan by poison, while the story of Husain's last expedition and his death in battle was embroidered with a wealth of pathetic detail.

Some seventy years after the battle of Karbala the explosion came in the shape of an uprising which utterly destroyed the Omayyad dynasty, all but annihilated that family, broke the Arab domination over Islam, and transferred the capital from Damascus to Mesopotamia, and eventually to Baghdad. The amazing part of the whole story is that though this revolution was in the main the work of the Shias, it did not establish their party as the predominant sect in Islam, nor did it call the descendants of Ali to the throne.

Abdallah, father of the Prophet Mohammed, had an elder brother named Abbas, as well as a younger brother, Abu Talib, who was the father of Ali. A son of this Abbas, by name Abdallah (the names recur in bewildering fashion in the pedigree of this family), held Basra as Viceroy for Ali at the time of that Caliph's assassination. He was in command of the army raised to assert the claims of Hassan against Moawiya, and was accused of having made good terms for himself even before Hassan abandoned the struggle. At any rate he retired to Mecca, taking with him the contents of the treasury at Basra. From this time the descendants of Abbas hung, as it were, on the flank of the Shia movement. They were admitted to its secrets, did their full share of the propaganda which turned Mohammedan opinion against the Omayyad dynasty, and seem generally to have been reckoned as partisans of the house of Ali; but they had claims of their own which they were prepared to assert if opportunity offered. One circumstance certainly worked in their favour. After the fall of Husain a large section of the Shias acclaimed as Imam a younger brother of his who was a son of Ali by another wife, and, therefore, not a grandson of the Prophet. To do this was to abandon the principle that the spiritual and temporal Headship of Islam was hereditary in the direct line of its Founder: if it were once acknowledged that any member of the Prophet's family might prove to be the divinely ordained Imam, then the descendants of Abbas could claim that they represented a senior line to that of the descendants of Ali. When the crisis came, a grandson of Abdallah, son of Abbas—his name was also Abdallah, but he assumed the designation of Abul Abbas,—proved to be a man altogether superior in ability and ruthless daring to Jafar, the great-grandson of Husain, who then represented the line of descent from Ali. By adroitly seizing his opportunity, Abul Abbas contrived to oust the line of Ali and secure the prize for himself. He founded the long line of Abbasid Caliphs who for centuries swayed the destinies of Islam from the splendid capital they built for themselves at Baghdad. Harun-al-Rashid, the hero of the 'Arabian Nights,' was the fifth Caliph of this line.

One can now begin to understand the environment in which the observance of the tenth day of Moharram, the anniversary of the death of Husain at Karbala, established itself as one of the great festivals of Islam. It was essentially Persian rather than Arabian in character, deriving some of its features from the passion plays or miracle plays which were popular in Persia in the days before the Moslem conquest. The early Caliphs of the Abbasid line owed much to the Shias; their accession had in fact recalled to orthodox

Islam great masses of what might be described as moderate Shia opinion. The extremists of that sect who still maintained that they owed allegiance to an Imam directly descended from Mohammed through his daughter, Fatima, secured a large measure of toleration; as between themselves and the new dynasty there was no desire on either side to force on an immediate quarrel. Moreover, the Abbasid Caliphs stood deeply committed to the campaign of vilification which had been carried on against the Omayyad dynasty. They could have no objection, for instance, to the growth of the legend that Hassan had been poisoned at the instigation of the Caliph of Damascus, or to the coupling of his name with that of Husain as a martyr who had fallen a victim to the malice of those oppressors of the family of the Prophet. The tomb of Husain was at Karbala, and there was no reason why it should not be permitted to become a place of pilgrimage and the scene of a passion-play, celebrated each year for several days at the commencement of the Moharram month, in which coffins of the 'martyrs' were carried in procession for solemn interment. The great mass of the Moslem population, ignorant of history and feeling no concern about dynastic quarrels which in any case were steadily receding into the mists of the past, accepted the festival as a solemn commemoration of the grandsons of the Prophet, who had been cut off in the flower of their age under circumstances into the precise nature of which it was quite unnecessary to inquire. In countries far removed from Iraq, and particularly in India, the celebration was limited —except amongst the extremists now definitely organised into the Shia sect—to a great procession on the tenth day of Moharram, in which what came to be called *tazias*, constructions of paper and tinsel on a framework of light bamboo, supposed to represent the tomb of Husain at Karbala, were carried through the streets of the great cities. The tradition that the whole celebration was in some way connected with the memory of a battle survived in a tendency to enliven the procession at intervals by displays of acrobatic sword-play, while its funeral character was preserved by a custom, usual but not invariable, of burying the *tazias* in some suitable plot of waste land at the conclusion of the procession.

As the years went by the Shias modified in one respect their doctrine regarding the headship of Islam. They reckoned up a line of twelve Imams in direct descent from Ali through Husain, down to a Mohammed surnamed the 'Mahdi'—the word means "he who is guided aright,"—in respect of whom they taught that he was not dead but had vanished from human sight, to be restored by God to his faithful followers when the time appointed should arrive. This development facilitated the establishment of the Shia faith as the predominant form of Islam in the country which had always been its stronghold. When the empire of the Abbasid Caliphs crumbled under the assaults of the Turks, and Islamic countries organised themselves into separate kingdoms, nothing remained of the Caliphate but a claim to a sort of spiritual primacy in matters of faith. For a long time this was understood to attach to descendants of the Abbasid line residing in Egypt, but the last Caliph of this line was captured by the Turkish Sultan, Selim I., in 1517. The orthodox view then became that the Caliphate had passed to the sultans of Turkey by voluntary surrender, their claim being strengthened by their control over the Holy Places of Arabia. The Shahs of Persia were not on good terms with the Turks, and in their own country they could claim a superior status as Viceregents of the absent Imam. The Shia faith, thus established in Persia, obtained a footing in India in virtue of the fact that the ruling family of Oudh was of Persian descent and adhered to the ancestral form of belief.

Thus it comes about that the Shias, while a quite inconsiderable minority amongst the Moslems of India, muster strongly at Lucknow and one or two other places, and include a larger proportion of landed gentry and men of superior social position. They differ from their Sunni neighbours in certain details of civil and religious law, and it must be remembered that amongst Mohammedans generally there is no real distinction between civil law and religious law; but in practice the differences between Sunni and Shia are apt to be accentuated principally in their divergent attitudes towards the Moharram celebrations. With the Shias this is a period of mourning, commencing with the eighth day of the month D'hul Hijja, the day on which Husain set forth from Mecca at the head of his faithful adherents, and continuing beyond the tenth day of the Moharram month right on to the festival of the *Chehlum*, 'the fortieth day,' said to be the day on which the severed head of Husain, having been sent in token of triumph to the Caliph Yazid at Damascus, was returned for burial in his tomb at Karbala. The Shia legend is that the head had confounded the enemies of the Prophet's house by persistently working miracles, until it was so returned for honourable interment.

A special feature of the Shia celebrations during the entire period is the holding of *Majlises*, meetings at which books are read aloud in the hearing of the faithful, dealing with the story of the descendants of the Prophet and of Imam Husain in particular. It has been my privilege on various occasions to avail myself of the courtesy of an invitation to attend such a meeting. Seated in a quiet corner, I have looked across the dimly-lighted courtyard of some great house where the listeners sat absorbed, while the reader, his back turned to the majority of his audience, read in a loud voice from the volume before him. His voice rose and fell in a sort of chant, swaying the emotions of the entire gathering like a wind blowing over a field of ripe corn. At intervals some voice, usually that of an aged man, would break out in a cry of, "Alas! and woe is me for the grandson of the Prophet!"; and a wave of lamentation would break forth uncontrollably, subsiding again into silence as the reader resumed his recital. Fragments of the pathetic story linger in my memory. For instance, on the night before the battle, Husain, after vainly exhorting his faithful few to return to their homes and shed no blood in his defence, was resting alone in his tent, preparing himself by meditation and prayer to meet the fate awaiting him. Suddenly, a cloud gathering in a corner of the tent began to take shape and a visitor appeared. It was the King of the Djinns, converted long ago to Islam by the preaching of Mohammed, come to offer his services to the grandson of the Prophet in his hour of need. Let Husain but speak the word, and in the twinkling of an eye the opposing host, the followers of the usurper who presumed to call himself Caliph of Islam, would be swept out of existence. " And what," said Husain sadly, " shall I answer at the Day of Judgment when it is inquired of me who was responsible for the death of so many true believers ? " The King of the Djinns retired, weeping. The story of the next day's battle is full of details of the heroism displayed by Husain's devoted bodyguard. They were true Janissaries —*Jan Nisar*, the words mean 'Life Scatterer,' one ready to fling away his life as a thing of no account in defence of his lord. It is told how in the heat of the terrible day Husain was faint with thirst, and a handful of his defenders fought their way through the opposing host to fill for him a water-carrier's leathern bucket from the river, and the enemy who had failed to resist their onset contrived to frustrate their purpose by shooting it full of arrows as they bore it back. One is reminded of that other contest against overwhelming numbers, which lasted

> "Until King Arthur's Table, man by man,
> Had fallen in Lyonnese about their Lord";

but here there remained no faithful Sir Bedivere to carry the stricken hero from the field. His enemies had their will, though even amongst them old men shuddered as they looked upon the severed head, remembering that they had seen the dead lips pressed by those of the Prophet of God.

CHAPTER II.

MOHARRAM IN LUCKNOW.

LUCKNOW was the capital of the old kingdom of Oudh, and it has been explained that the royal family of Oudh adhered to the Shia faith of their Persian ancestors. As might be expected, the principal noblemen and office-bearers about the court belonged to the same sect. Nevertheless these gentlemen, and those of their dependants who elected to follow the form of faith accepted by their masters, never constituted anything but a minority amongst the Moslem population of the city. At the present day the Sunnis in Lucknow outnumber the Shias by considerably more than five to one. A peculiar feature of the position is, however, that the men of high social status—"the sort of people," as an indignant Sunni put it to me, "who are accommodated with chairs when they call on local officials"—are almost all Shias. The *Karbala*, as they called the enclosure to which, by long-established tradition, the *tazias* were carried at the end of the procession of the tenth day of Moharram, was in Shia hands, under the control of an association of influential gentlemen belonging to that sect. In Lucknow, therefore, if nowhere else in India, a devout Shia might hope to see the public celebration of the Moharram festival conducted in a fashion more in accordance with his own ideas of what was proper to the occasion. To him the procession of the *Ashra*—the tenth day of Moharram—came as the climax of a period of mourning, of abstinence from the ordinary pleasures of life, of meditation on the sufferings of the descendants of the Prophet. He desired to follow his *tazia* barefoot and bareheaded, with every outward demonstration of sorrow, as if he were, in imagination, following the corpses of the martyred Imams to their grave.

Now to the inhabitants of Lucknow generally, including Mohammedans of the lower orders, the butchers, weavers, and artisans constituting the rank and file of the Sunni party, the procession of the *Ashra* comes as an isolated event. It is a demonstration in honour of the grandsons of the Prophet, a declaration of enthusiastic adherence to the faith and of reverence for the memory of its founder. No doubt, in their minds also the tradition remains that the ceremony commemorates the deaths of Hassan and Husain, and is to this extent an occasion of mourning; but it is not in human nature to arrive at a passion of grief because a man who died over twelve hundred years ago is not still alive, unless the mind dwells upon the circumstances of his death as being in themselves tragic and utterly lamentable. This is precisely what a Shia can do in the case of Husain, and according to his tradition in that of Hassan as well, but a Sunni cannot. During the controversy which I am about to describe, a pamphleteer on the Shia side declared that, while the two sects were no doubt commemorating on the tenth of Moharram one and the same event, the battle of Karbala, the Shias lamented the sad fate of Husain, but the Sunnis exulted in the triumph of the army of Yazid. The remark gave deep offence at the time, and is in fact untrue; but educated Sunnis know that their position with regard to the Moharram celebrations is an illogical one, and the taunt rankled all the more for this very reason.

Moreover, it must be remembered that the Mohammedans of Lucknow are themselves a minority in the midst of a heathen population. The Hindus can understand readily enough a demonstration in which some object having religious significance is carried in procession; but to them such a procession would be a festival, a holiday to be celebrated with all the usual concomitants of one of their own fairs. Obviously nothing can prevent them from gathering in thousands to watch the procession of *tazias*, and in Lucknow they have actually been allowed a certain participation in the ceremony itself. Presumably some Hindu official in the service of the King of Oudh, or some Hindu retainer of a Mohammedan family, must in the first instance have petitioned for permission to display his respect for the religious beliefs and traditions of his master by himself contributing a *tazia* to the display. At any rate, it has become an established custom that in the Lucknow celebrations there are 'Shia *tazias*,' 'Sunni *tazias*,' and 'Hindu *tazias*,' and up to a certain time these followed one another indiscriminately along the traditional routes, converging upon the Shia *Karbala*. This necessarily accentuated the tendency to obscure the Shia view of the entire demonstration as an act of solemn mourning, and to introduce features associated with an ordinary popular festivity. The precincts of the Karbala took on more and more the aspect of a fair-ground. Stalls and booths for the sale of refreshments to the weary followers of the procession were perhaps a necessity; but the inevitable tendency would be to set up booths for the sale of any articles which could be disposed of to advantage at an ordinary fair. Then enterprising speculators brought in swings and merry-go-rounds, for the entertainment of such spectators, Hindu or Moslem, as might be ready to seek pleasure therein. On the top of everything else an abuse crept in which could not be defended by any honest Moslem, and was frankly intolerable to the devout Shia. Lucknow is a gay city, with a tradition of dissolute manners surviving from the days when its native dynasty was falling into decay. The ladies of what Rudyard Kipling calls the most ancient profession in the world began to seek their opportunity in the coming together of a festival throng; they set up booths of their own at and about the terminus of the procession, if not in the *Karbala* itself. There were thus abundant materials to attract the attention of a Puritan reformer, and some action was inevitable if anything should occur to stir the leading gentlemen of the Shia faith out of their attitude of tolerant acquiescence in established things.

The impulse came during the years 1904–5, in the preaching of a fanatic named Maqbul Ahmad, and a controversy which he stirred up with rival exponents of the Sunni faith regarding the distinctive tenets of the two sects. Now it is one of the difficulties of our position in India that any movement which strongly excites the religious feelings of any section of the population is apt to create trouble for those responsible for the maintenance of public order. We have to deal with religions closely interwoven into the texture of everyday life, with people strongly susceptible to religious emotion and always inclined

> "To prove their doctrine orthodox
> By apostolic blows and knocks."

Nor can it be denied that there are always mischief-makers abroad, ready to intermeddle in any matter for the mere sake of stirring up trouble. Yet it has often appeared to me that the root of the difficulty strikes deeper and is inherent in the position of a Government which claims to stand aloof from, and hold an even balance between, all forms of religious belief. We are pledged to maintain all sections of the population in the free exercise of their several religions; the tendency is to interpret this pledge in such a manner as to make the British Government the defender and supporter of all established things. Sometimes the vested interests which appeal to the Government for support are not intrinsically deserving of it; they may have sprung from nothing better than the tendency towards corruption and decay inherent in long-established things. It may require all the insight and tact and firmness of a great administrator, like the gentleman who lately laid down the Governorship of the Panjab, to hold the balance even between sympathy for a reforming movement directed against undoubted abuses, and insistence on the principle that reform must not be effected by violence outside the limits of the law. Even in the sphere of legislation the Government often finds itself in a difficulty when appealed to by contending parties to throw its weight either on the side of a movement of social reform, or on the side of the orthodox supporters of things as they are. I am not as sure as I should like to be that there is no foundation for the occasional complaints of earnest social reformers that a policy of neutrality, even of benevolent neutrality, on the part of Government may prove a decisive obstacle in their way. I must not be tempted to proceed further with this digression; but I have often thought how close a parallel might arise between the position of a certain sorely tried Roman administrator in Palestine some nineteen hundred years ago, and that of an English Magistrate, let us say in Benares, called upon at short notice to deal with disturbances threatened by the preaching of a Hindu Reformer who had been denouncing caste restrictions and throwing doubt on the efficacy of a bath in the sacred river for the purification of sins.

The trouble in Lucknow, of which I am tracing the history, was not a very important affair. Sir John Hewett, in his retirement, probably regards it as one of the minor episodes of his very successful Lieutenant-Governorship; but events might easily have taken a different course if the matter had been handled with less insight and firmness. In the end the Lieutenant-Governor was brought up against the old problem, whether an act of plain justice towards a weak minority should be carried through at the risk of having to use force to repress the fanaticism of the strong. I have to show how it was faced.

The question was complicated by the fact that the Shias of Lucknow went considerably out of their way to ask for trouble. The controversy stirred up by the preaching of Maqbul Ahmad roused them to an insistence on their peculiar views regarding the Moharram observances generally. They could point to undoubted abuses which called for correction, but they endeavoured to take advantage of this fact in order to impose upon a Moslem community in which they themselves constituted a small minority their own methods of observance, and in particular their own attitude towards the procession of the tenth of Moharram. They began with the *Chehlum* festival of 1905, the 'fortieth day' festival which closed the period of mourning for that year. This being a matter in which the great mass of the Sunnis took little interest, they had no difficulty in securing official sanction for their proposed reforms and bringing the observances of that day more or less into accordance with their own ideas. In due course the Moharram period of 1906 came round, and the District Magistrate was called upon to issue the usual proclamation regulating the great procession of the *Ashra*. The Shias succeeded in obtaining from him an order they had long desired, prohibiting all displays of swordplay and similar amusements which the Sunnis of the lower orders had come to regard as one of the most interesting features of the holiday. This was enough to set flying a whole crop of rumours calculated to aggravate the situation. There was a regulation against 'improper behaviour' within the precincts of the Karbala, which was distorted by mischief-makers into an assertion that the Shia gentlemen who controlled this place had been given authority to eject anyone whose conduct at the terminus of the procession did not square with their notions of what was befitting to the occasion. In particular, it was alleged that no one would be allowed to enter the Karbala who had not followed his *tazia* with bare head and feet, after the Shia fashion. Feelings had begun to warm up on both sides, and there were probably fanatics on the Shia side prepared to enforce such a regulation as a fit and proper one to be made, whether or not it had official authority behind it.

All the materials seemed to be collected for a nasty explosion, but the prospect of a faction-fight on a large scale in the streets of Lucknow was not one which any responsible person could contemplate with equanimity. At almost the last possible moment the District Magistrate was approached by some of the leading Sunnis with the suggestion that the only way of averting a serious disturbance would be to allow the Sunnis to start a *Karbala* of their own. One of them offered to dedicate for the purpose a plot of waste land which was conveniently situated, in that it lay on the outskirts of the town, in a different direction from that of the customary terminus of the procession. What was requested was a Magistrate's order authorising its use, and a proclamation to be made immediately by beat of drum in all quarters of the city, that any persons so desiring were at liberty to take their *tazias* along a prescribed route to the new terminus. The arrangement was sanctioned, but it came out afterwards that in many quarters of the town the proclamation actually made was that all 'Sunni *tazias*' and 'Hindu *tazias*' must proceed to the new *Karbala*. It proved in the end that the fanatics on both sides had unintentionally co-operated towards one and the same result. The zeal of the Puritan reformers on the Shia side, striving to secure that all *tazias* approaching the traditional terminus should be escorted by companies of genuine mourners, helped to divert the Sunni and Hindu *tazias* towards the new route; while religious leaders amongst the Sunnis were by this time fully awake to the possible advantages of having a *Karbala* of their own, free from any tradition of Shia control. The celebration of the *Ashra* passed off without any disturbance, but it ended in a definite cleavage, every single *tazia* being now classified as having passed under the control either of the Sunnis or of the Shias.

Neither side was really satisfied with the result. The Shias were in a position to see that the proceedings at their ancient Karbala were conducted in accordance with their own ideas of what befitted the occasion, but the place was shorn of much of its ancient glory. It had become the rendezvous of a sect instead of a meeting-place for the united forces of Islam. On the other hand the Sunnis of the lower orders felt that they had been hustled away into the wilderness and their customary festivity deprived, for the time being at any rate, of many of its wonted amenities. The Shias would now have been prepared to make large concessions for the sake of bringing back all the *tazias* once more to the traditional terminus, but the next move was clearly with the Sunnis. Would they come to terms, or would they follow the leadership of men who looked upon the rupture with complacency and envisaged the possibility of something in the nature of a distinctively Sunni Moharram?

The answer developed itself gradually in the course of the following year. As the reader will see presently, I had better opportunities than most men for investigating the facts; yet I have never been able to make up my mind how far the subsequent course of events represented the outcome of a scheme formulated by some organiser of genius on the Sunni side, from the moment that permission was sought for the institution of the new *Karbala,* and how far things simply evolved spontaneously under the pressure of partisan feeling. I know that the besetting weakness of an English official who sets himself to discover what is really going on under the surface of Indian life, is to fancy that he can see farther through a stone wall than most men. There was once a Deputy Commissioner in my part of India whose epitaph, after his retirement, was pronounced by one of the wittiest of after-dinner speakers describing him as: "the Fouché of our service; whose boast it was to know everything that happened in his district—and a great many things that didn't." In this particular matter I thought myself for a time hot upon the scent of a Sunni plot of the most elaborate description, but in the long-run I was inclined to accuse myself of allowing imagination to work ahead of the facts. Given the actual situation and the state of feeling on both sides, the general trend of events was predetermined; no artistry other than that inherent in a popular movement was needed to give them the curious and interesting shape they finally assumed.

The resentment of the Sunni populace against the Puritan Shias who had assailed their method of celebrating the *Ashra* festival found vent in the growth and development of a popular hymnology, songs, and verses in honour of the *Chār Yār*—the 'Four Comrades,'—by whom they meant the first four Caliphs, Abu Bakr, Omar, Usman, and Ali. The words were in themselves a direct challenge. According to the Shias, Ali had been designated by Mohammed himself as his immediate successor; he was the rightful Imam, the spiritual and temporal Head of Islam, from the moment of the Prophet's death. Abu Bakr, Omar, and Usman were tyrants and usurpers, reprobated by every true Shia in a formula so offensive to the ears of the orthodox Sunni that its public use had to be restrained by judicial decisions. As against this, the entire Sunni case was summed up in the formula, 'The Four Comrades,' friends and comrades alike of the Prophet and of one another. It implied that the Shias were setting up on behalf of Ali a claim which he had himself repudiated when he acquiesced in the successive elections to the Caliphate of Abu Bakr, Omar, and Usman. And, of course, there was much to say in praise of these ancient worthies. Abu Bakr was acclaimed as the close friend and counsellor of the Prophet, the man who had saved the Faith at the crisis caused by the death of its Founder, and had afterwards collected the words of the sacred book, the Koran, from the scattered records in which the sacred pages had been preserved and from the lips of those who had gotten them by heart. Omar was the 'Slayer of the infidel,' the great commander who had launched Islam on its career of conquest. Usman had fixed the authoritative text of the Koran, when it was in danger of being perpetuated in variant versions, and his death at the hands of mutinous subjects furnished his cause with a martyr whose story could be set against the Shia lamentations for the fate of Ali and his descendants. No Orangeman, toasting the pious and immortal memory of King William before a gathering of his Romanist fellow-countrymen, could enjoy an experience quite so satisfying as that of the enthusiastic Sunni chanting the praises of his heroes in the hearing of heretic Shias. Moreover, the Sunni had a peculiar pleasure in reserve. When he had goaded every Shia within hearing to fury by his praises of the men whom they called tyrants and usurpers, he could, serenely pursuing his chosen theme, issue to the heretics the invitation and the challenge to join with him in acclaiming their common hero, Ali, the beloved son-in-law of the Prophet, the victorious champion of Islam in its hour of direst peril; and so pass on to sum up the argument in some cheerful refrain, declaring that "the Banner of the Four Holy Comrades is securely planted in all four corners of the world." Indeed, he had sharper and more venomous arrows than this in his quiver. The refrain of one of the 'Charyari' songs concluded its glorification of the four Comrades with a pungent quatrain of which the following is an inadequate version :—

> "All these four were, heart and soul, defenders of the Right;
> He who loves them loves indeed God's Messenger as well.
> The wretch who bears towards one of these enmity or spite,
> By Mohammed's own decree is doomed—is doomed to hell!"

I have listened to some curious pieces of dialectic in my time, but I was never quite so taken aback as when a learned and respected priest of the Sunnis appealed to me to say whether it was not a bit perverse on the part of the Shias to take exception to the above lines. The verse, he contended, said "*one* of these"; it did not specify which one. Why were not the Shias content to assume that the one referred to (and the only one) was their own hero, Ali?

The *Charyari* verses came in gradually; they were published in little leaflets and eagerly committed to memory by illiterate butchers and artisans. The next move was that groups of exultant Sunnis, following their own *tazias* in the *Ashra* procession, would break out at intervals into one or other of these popular refrains. All question of bringing back the 'Sunni *tazias*' to the ancient terminus was at once precluded. Indeed, it became increasingly obvious that the cleavage in the Moharram celebrations would have to go further than the mere institution of two separate *Karbalas*. If, during the earlier part of the procession, a *tazia* escorted by a band of Shia mourners were to find itself sandwiched in between two others the followers of which were Sunnis, the latter chanting even one of the less objectionable of the *Charyari* refrains, there would be the risk of a serious collision. The Moharram celebrations of 1907 passed off in an atmosphere of grave and increasing tension. All sorts of efforts were made to bring responsible leaders of the two parties together and help them to work out the terms of a settlement. One after another these broke down. The *Charyari* verses had captivated the Sunnis of the lower orders; the matter was passing out of the control of their leaders. On the *Ashra* day of 1908 there was a nasty riot, which only failed to reach really dangerous proportions because the Shias were, after all, in a hopeless minority. Probably also their leaders were able to exercise sufficient control to limit the disturbances to what was necessary to force on the attention of those in authority the undoubted fact that the Shias could not tolerate the further development of a movement which was perverting the whole meaning and purpose of the procession of the tenth of Moharram into a Sunni demonstration.

Something had to be done before the Moharram of 1909 came round, and the Lieutenant-Governor took the matter into his own hands. He began by appointing a small Committee to investigate and report. I have never deluded myself into the belief that my appointment to the Chairmanship of this Committee was due to anything more than the fact that certain accidents of the service had left me more or less at a loose end that cold weather. An officer of a certain status was required, and I happened to be the one whose services were most readily available. It was a fortunate accident which gave me four or five of the most interesting weeks of my Indian career. The Committee included one other Englishman, a non-official chosen because of his long residence in Lucknow and the respect he commanded amongst all classes, two Hindu gentlemen to act as impartial arbitrators and to enforce by their presence the fact that the celebration of the Moharram was a matter which concerned all the citizens of Lucknow, and two representatives each from the Sunnis and the Shias respectively, including in each case one of the religious leaders of the community.

I have always counted myself fortunate in the possession of Indian friends who did not mind telling me the truth ; so it came about that before the Committee met I knew that its appointment had been received with something very like derision by the Mohammedans of Lucknow generally. Their attitude was summed up in a remark which reached my ears. "This dispute," said a certain gentleman, referring generally to the differences between Sunnis and Shias, "has been going on for more than twelve hundred years : does Piggott Sahib suppose that he is going to settle it in two or three weeks ?" I need hardly say that I never entertained any such ambition. The first business of the Committee was to ascertain the facts, and more particularly to place it beyond doubt how far the existing tension between the contending parties was due to innovations introduced by either of them into the ancient and established routine of the Moharram celebrations. Then the bringing together of responsible leaders from each of the two communities, to discuss their differences across a table in the presence of disinterested arbitrators, might be expected at least to clarify the issues, narrowing down the area of the dispute to the barest essentials. It was at least possible that this process might be carried down to a point which left nothing in respect of which a compromise acceptable to both parties could not be arranged. If this was too much to expect, there would remain the fact that no responsible person on either side wanted to see the streets of Lucknow in the possession of a raging mob and the military called in to preserve order : it was, therefore, possible that the Committee might arrive at unanimity in recommending particular measures as essential to the preservation of the public peace. Failing this again, the four arbitrators could at least formulate their recommendations, leaving it to the Sunni and Shia members respectively to state precisely which of these they were unable to accept, and to give reasons for their inability.

This was pretty much what happened in the long-run, but our investigations covered much interesting ground. There were matters of detail upon which a compromise was actually reached. For instance, we were able to nip in the bud a practice which zealous partisans on both sides had been trying to introduce, of carrying along with the *tazias* certain flags or streamers bearing inscriptions; both sides agreed that this was an objectionable innovation, each accusing the other of being responsible for it. When the Sunni and Shia members both agreed that a formal prohibition of any such practice might well be inserted in the Magistrate's proclamation regulating the proceedings at the next Moharram, a point had been gained of which the full significance only became apparent later. It was now common ground that a detail of this sort could be regulated by executive proclamation. Nor was either party prepared to deny that the District Magistrate had authority to regulate the route or routes to be followed by the procession. It must be remembered that each individual *tazia* had its traditional starting-point from which it must be carried to join the main stream. The Shia members would have been glad enough to secure a delimitation of routes involving the abolition of the new Sunni *Karbala* and the return of all the *tazias* to the traditional terminus, but even they tacitly admitted that this was impossible unless some compromise could be reached on the subject of the *Charyari* songs.

Here we came to an impasse. We went carefully into the history of the matter. Little printed books and leaflets containing the verses were laid upon the table, and evidence was collected as to their dates. Witnesses were examined as to the extent to which the chanting of these verses had become a feature of the Moharram processions, and the earliest date from which any such practice could be said to have commenced. The case for the Shias was that some of these verses constituted a deliberate and calculated insult to their religion, so gross that their utterance in a public place and in the hearing of Shia believers constituted in itself an offence against the common law. The praises of Abu Bakr, Omar, and Usman, were in themselves a provocation to any devout Shia, who must not be blamed if the sound of them moved him to retort with his formula of reprobation the utterance of which was treated by the Sunnis as an intolerable insult. In any case, the use made of the *Charyari* verses during the last Moharram distorted the entire meaning and purpose of the ceremony, turning it from a commemoration of the martyred grandsons of the

Prophet into a demonstration in favour of the cardinal doctrine of the Sunni faith. The case for the Sunnis was that every true believer had an inherent right to laud and magnify in public, in such manner as he might think most fitting, the traditional heroes of his faith. The public chanting or recitation of these *Charyari* verses either was an offence against the common law or it was not. Let those who alleged it to be such an offence bring the matter to the test of a public prosecution ; every religious-minded Sunni understood the duty of obeying the law of the land in which he lived, and they would submit to the decision of the courts. If, however, there was no offence against the ordinary law, what right had the District Magistrate to proclaim that it should be deemed a punishable offence in particular circumstances ?

And so the High Priest of the Shias drew his dark mantle around him and withdrew into the attitude of one absorbed in meditation upon higher things. This, indeed, he had preserved throughout the proceedings of the Committee, only departing from it at intervals to pronounce, with an air of ultimate finality which the Roman Pontiff might have envied, a few terse sentences defining the Shia attitude on some controverted point. The keen-eyed Maulavi of the Sunnis looked hard at the Chairman, and trusted that no ill-advised action on the part of the Government would suggest to the great mass of humble, but zealous, Moslems the perilous suspicion that they were being hindered in the free exercise of their religion. The independent members of the Committee were agreed as to what ought to be done, and left it to the Chairman to put their ideas into shape. When the draft report was laid on the table, the Sunni and Shia members alike asked for a week's time in which to consider so important a document. It would be impossible for them to sign it as it stood; perhaps they might be permitted to formulate in writing the points on which they dissented and their reasons for doing so?

There seemed nothing more to be done. I adjourned the Committee to that day week and returned to my own quarters, speculating on the possibility of a little shooting-trip for myself into one of the sub-montane districts of Oudh. I had reckoned without the shrewd vigilance of the Lieutenant-Governor. He was at Allahabad at the time, a night's journey from Lucknow by train. I was sitting down to dinner, possibly four hours after the adjournment of the Committee, when a telegram was put into my hands. The wording of that telegram became one of those minor jests which brighten the tedium of official life. At Allahabad the problem had been how to communicate with me and not risk setting the busy tongue of irresponsible rumour awag; I did not possess the official cipher. The Chief Secretary, however, was an old friend and had not forgotten the days when we were at the House together. This is what I read:—

"Ean hoi boulomenoi ouk homologousin su autos en taute te nukti panta ta gegrammena phere."

It may not have been classical Greek, but it served. I collected my *dossier* and left for Allahabad by the night train. About six in the morning I handed in the file to the Chief Secretary and told him how matters stood. I saw the Lieutenant-Governor soon after eleven. The first question or two which he put to me showed that he had found time enough to learn everything which it was in the least important that he should know, had sifted out the essentials of the problem and saw his way towards its solution. I was back in Lucknow before anyone can have begun to gossip concerning my absence, and I had put in quite a pleasant shooting-trip before I met the Committee again.

The dissentient memoranda signed respectively by the two Sunni and the two Shia members were at once laid on the table. The other half of the Committee had awaited the same with some anxiety, but when we came to go through them our principal feeling was one of relief. Both were lengthy documents, the Sunni memorandum portentously so, but they made it clear enough that the essential controversy had been brought within narrow limits. Our majority report had recommended official action in two important directions. In the first place, the cleavage in the Moharram celebrations was recognised as an accomplished fact. It was suggested that it should be carried to its logical conclusion, and the risk of collision reduced to a minimum, by official orders prescribing separate routes and separate times for the two processions directed respectively towards the Sunni and the Shia *Karbala*. In the second place, with regard to the *Charyari* verses, we recommended that the Magistrate's order should prohibit the chanting or recitation of such verses by demonstrators accompanying the *tazias*, or along the prescribed routes of the processions, or within the hearing of processions moving along the said routes. The sum and substance of the Sunni memorial was that any such prohibition would amount to interference with the free exercise of religion, and was beyond the competence of the District Magistrate. On the other side the Shias pressed for a general prohibition of the public singing or recitation of *Charyari* verses throughout the whole of what they regarded as the 'Moharram period,' extending for two months, or rather more, right down to the festival of the 'fortieth day.' Their main argument was that it would not be found possible to frame any prohibition short of this, and not leave loopholes for evasion of which advantage would be taken by evil-disposed persons. I am free to admit that I was so impressed with this argument that my own opinion had wavered in the direction of some attempt to meet the wishes of the Shia minority in this matter. It was fortunate, as the event proved, that I had with me on the Committee a Hindu lawyer of sound judgment and wide experience. His exposition, both of the common law against intentional insult to the religious feelings of others and of the limits of the Magistrate's powers in the regulation of public meetings and processions, had been masterly; it rightly determined the substance of the main report on this point.

I got this report and the two dissentient memoranda duly signed, collected all the records of the Committee's proceedings, and once more took train for Allahabad. There the matter was finally threshed out with the Chief Secretary and the Lieutenant-Governor. Well in advance of the advent of the Moharram period of 1909, the full report of the Committee was published in the 'Gazette' of the province, with a Government Resolution reviewing the same and clearly defining the action proposed to be taken. There was ample time for any persons dissatisfied with the result to lay their grievances before the Government of India, by way of petition or memorial. What use was made of the opportunity was no concern of mine.

On the *Ashra* day of 1909 the Magistrate's orders regulating the processions were on the lines suggested in the report of the majority of the Committee. The arrangements made by the local authorities for the preservation of public order were overwhelmingly complete. What might have happened had they been otherwise, must remain matter for conjecture. What actually occurred was a slight disturbance, just sufficient, and no more, to serve as a formal challenge to the validity of the Magistrate's orders. A handful of Sunni demonstrators, following one of their *tazias*, broke out into one of the forbidden chants. They were at once hemmed in by a strong force of police and shepherded into the courtyard of the nearest police station, where they were only detained until they had given their names and addresses and entered into recognisances to appear when called upon.

The test case which followed was taken right up to the highest court of appeal, the question of the District Magistrate's powers in the regulation of processions and gatherings in the public streets being thoroughly threshed out. Learned counsel for the accused inquired indignantly whether the Court would uphold the Magistrate's action if, for instance, he were to issue an order that all persons following one of the *tazias* in procession must do so on their hands and knees. The Judicial Commissioner drily remarked that the Court would deal with such a contingency, if and when it arose. This was accepted as an admission that the discretion of the Magistrate was not absolute; the Court had jurisdiction to consider the reasonableness and propriety of his orders. This proposition the prosecution was prepared to concede, subject only to the qualification that the Magistrate on whom lay the responsibility for the maintenance of public order and security must be allowed a wide discretion, so long as he acted in good faith and with this object alone in view. In the particular case before the Court there was no real answer to the position taken up in the Government Resolution which lay behind the Magistrate's order. However acceptable to all or to some the praises of the first four Caliphs might be, their public recitation in connection with the Moharram processions was out of place. Not merely was it an innovation forming no part of the customary and established routine of the celebration, but it was essentially alien to its spirit and purpose. The systematic use of the *Charyari* verses distorted the entire ceremonial of the Moharram into something which it was not historically, never had been and was never intended to be. It was, moreover, highly offensive to the susceptibilities of a section which, though a minority, happened to be the one most interested in the celebration. It could scarcely be denied that its recent use in Lucknow had been intentionally provocative; in the interests of the public peace the thing had to be prohibited altogether.

The decision of the Judicial Commissioner's Court, upholding the action of the District Magistrate, proved the conclusion of the matter. To the credit of the Sunnis of Lucknow and their leaders it must be said that they submitted to the decision of the Courts of Law. Twenty years have now gone by—had the interval been less, I might have hesitated to revive the memory of the controversy,—but I think the *Charyari* verses may now be given their modest niche in the temple of history.

CHAPTER III.

MOHARRAM IN AMROHA.

THE district of Moradabad, like that of Budaun, represents a fragment of the old Rohilla monarchy which passed to the British by cession from the Nawab of Oudh. The name of its principal city, the headquarters station of Moradabad, recalls the gallant and ill-fated Prince Murad, the youngest son of the Emperor Shah Jehan, who fell a victim to the treachery of his elder brother Aurangzeb. The district as a whole contains a larger proportion of Mohammedans than any other in the province; they form more than one-third of the total population. It is peculiar also in comprising at least three other towns of considerable size besides Moradabad itself. One of these is Amroha, an old town which has seen better days, but can still boast a population of over forty thousand souls, and the possession of the tomb of a famous Moslem saint. It so happens, moreover, that a number of the leading landholders of the place belong to old families which adhere to the Shia faith. In many respects, therefore, the position in Amroha with regard to the Moharram celebrations reproduces on a smaller scale features which have already been noticed in connection with Lucknow.

The story I have to tell may serve to illustrate

one of the problems which from time to time confront the British administration in India—namely, the difficulty of exercising effective control in places not merely at a distance from the provincial capital, but away from district headquarters. The general custom was for the Joint Magistrate of Moradabad to proceed to Amroha a day or two before the procession of the *Ashra*, and take charge of the arrangements; but on a certain year early in the present century the Joint Magistrate was urgently wanted elsewhere. The District Magistrate, himself necessarily tied to Moradabad for the period of the festival, did the best thing possible under the circumstances by selecting from amongst his deputies a senior officer of experience, himself a Mohammedan, and putting him in charge of the celebration at Amroha. He had no reason to concern himself beforehand either with the social status or the religious beliefs of the officer in question; but that gentleman was a Sunni Mohammedan, and was, moreover, what we should regard in England as a self-made man. That is to say he had risen, by his own superior abilities, from a comparatively humble class of Mohammedan society, a class with a certain reputation for holding with peculiar zeal and tenacity the distinguishing tenets of their religious faith. It may be observed also that it was quite in accordance with the fitness of things that the leading executive officials posted for residence at a place like Amroha should be Mohammedans, and if so they would in all probability be adherents of the faith held by the vast majority of Indian Moslems. As a matter of fact, at the time in question, the *Tahsildar* (the Revenue Officer and petty Magistrate) and the Inspector of Police at Amroha were both Sunnis. I do not suppose that the possibility of any inconvenience arising from this fact ever crossed the mind of the District Magistrate at Moradabad; and even if it had done so, he could do no more than manage his district with the staff at his disposal. Nevertheless the fact remains that the Moharram arrangements at Amroha were left in charge of three Sunnis, with at their head an officer whom the Shia gentry of the place might, at a critical moment, just take it into their heads to distrust.

The Deputy Magistrate took up his residence in the heart of the town in a large house placed at his disposal by a gentleman of the place. In view of what followed the situation of this house is important. Its frontage was upon a narrow lane, on to which its outer courtyard opened by a wide gateway, fitted with tall and substantial wooden doors. Anyone turning to his left on leaving this gateway would arrive, in twenty or thirty paces, at one of the main streets of the city, into which the lane debouched at right angles. The other end of the lane was a cul-de-sac, ending in a blank wall. There were no shops along the lane; the only other doors opening into it were the narrow entrances of private houses belonging to Hindus of the class of shopkeepers or small traders.

The first hint of impending trouble came in the shape of a petition laid before the Deputy Magistrate a couple of days before the date fixed for the great procession of the *Ashra*. The petitioner was a Hindu of a respectable middle-class family. He represented that there was a wedding to take place at his house, and the astrologers responsible for choosing an auspicious day had fixed upon a date which he was informed corresponded with the tenth day of the Mohammedan month of Moharram. As his house was not on the route to be taken by the procession of *tazias*, nor even in close proximity to that route, he had not at first thought the question of the date of any particular importance. It now occurred to him that his small wedding procession, accompanied by such music or other display of rejoicing as might fit the occasion, must at some point or other traverse the route taken by the *tazias*, and might even have to proceed along it for a short distance. He prayed that suitable arrangements might be made to safeguard his procession from any interference on the part of the Mohammedans, and that formal sanction might be accorded for the festivity he proposed to celebrate.

In all the proceedings that followed, the good faith of the petitioner was never called in question; at least it was never challenged in open court. No one doubted that the petitioner was prepared with overwhelming evidence that he had consulted the right persons before fixing the date of the wedding, and that they had found the day which corresponded with the *Ashra* of the Mohammedans to be the only possible auspicious day available anywhere near the time desired. Nevertheless I take leave to doubt whether that petition would have been presented at all if the English Joint Magistrate had been in charge of the Moharram arrangements. If it had, it would have been at once returned, to be rewritten and tendered in a substantially altered form. On the day of the *Ashra* the streets of Amroha, and more particularly those forming the traditional route of the procession of *tazias*, were under the jurisdiction of the Magistrate, for him to regulate what should or should not be done therein, with due regard to the public security and the traditional rights of the Mohammedans in celebrating one of the great festivals of their religion. I know the gentleman who filled the office of Joint Magistrate at Moradabad during the greater part of my time there, quite well enough to form a pretty accurate mental picture of his attitude towards a Hindu merchant approaching him with a petition to be allowed to conduct a wedding procession through the streets of Amroha on that particular day of all the year. To start with, he would have overwhelmed the petitioner with condolences on the grave misfortune which had befallen him, in that the astrologers had been unable to find any other auspicious date. A shrewd hint would not have been omitted, that astrologers had been known to reconsider such a question, if it could be made worth their while to spend a little of their doubtless very valuable time in doing so. Failing this, of course, one must see what could be done. Obviously the traditional procession of the *tazias* had paramount claims; neither its route, nor the fairly wide limits of its appointed hours, could be subjected to the slightest interference. Naturally the Magistrate would be most reluctant to go the length of prohibiting a Hindu wedding procession on the *Ashra* day; but it might be necessary for him to fix a route for that procession involving a wide détour, or to limit it within hours which the petitioner might find none too convenient. Of course, the *Tahsildar* would be consulted; and if the petitioner would come round again that time to-morrow, he would be told what was the very best that could be done for him. In any case, it was to be hoped he would duly consider the trouble and inconvenience he was causing by not having given the authorities longer notice. In all probability the result of such an admonition would have been the reappearance of the petitioner with the joyful news that the astrologers had found another auspicious day. In any case the local Moslems would have heard the story with grim amusement, and no Hindu could have found valid reason for taking offence at the Magistrate's attitude.

Now I trust none of my readers will begin to suspect me at this point of a piece of insidious propaganda against the policy often referred to as the "Indianisation of the Services." I have long advocated the increased employment of

Indians in the service of their own country, and their promotion to posts of the highest responsibility. No problem, however, is brought a single step nearer to solution by the deliberate ignoring of its difficulties. This particular problem requires for its solution, on the British side, breadth of outlook and a readiness to accept reasonable risks for a worthy end; on the Indian side it calls for the growth of the spirit of citizenship, by which men will increasingly learn to regard themselves as Indians first, and Hindus or Moslems afterwards. A nation which aspires to govern itself must realise itself as a nation. I also ask readers to remember that the events of which I am writing happened more than a quarter of a century ago.

This much premised, I may without offence to anyone be allowed to note that the Deputy Magistrate, confronted with this petition, was at a disadvantage as compared with an English Joint Magistrate, whose absolute impartiality in the matter was certain, in any event, to pass unchallenged. The thing might be a test case, with influential Hindus in the background, waiting to raise an outcry that Hindu residents of Amroha were being denied by an intolerant Moslem official the ordinary rights of citizenship. On the other side the Deputy Magistrate could not fail to know that his proceedings were being keenly watched by co-religionists, who in their hearts trusted that he would regard himself as fortunate in that his position of authority enabled him to protect their rights and assert the dignity of the true faith.

He is in no way to be blamed for desiring to avail himself of the local knowledge and experience of his immediate subordinate, the *Tahsildar* of Amroha. What he failed to realise was the absolute necessity of promptitude in dealing with the question. His consultation of the *Tahsildar* needed to be an informal one, if it was to produce a speedy decision; moreover, the wording of the petition as a whole was, whether intentionally or otherwise, subtly provocative. It called for an immediate and unhesitating pronouncement as to the attitude of the responsible officer towards the question generally. It was never suggested afterwards, by the Deputy Magistrate or by anyone else, that he made any such pronouncement; what he did was to endorse the petition with a formal order referring it to the *Tahsildar* for report. More unhappily still, the *Tahsildar* passed a further order calling for a report from the Inspector of Police.

The actual result was that the petition was only disposed of, some forty-eight hours after its presentation, on the very eve of the *Ashra* procession. I really forget what were the precise orders eventually passed; I do know that I agreed with all other superior authorities in holding that those orders were quite unobjectionable, and would in all probability have been effective, if only they had not taken so long to prepare. The efforts I made later on to follow the course of events as they must have appeared to the eyes of the Shia gentlemen of Amroha were made under conditions which precluded complete success. Their attitude must have been determined by pre-existing circumstances, by something in the atmosphere of the place, never fully explained. The one certain thing is that they looked upon the presentation of the Hindu trader's petition, and its bandying about from one Sunni official to another, with the gravest suspicion. The time came when I found myself questioning the most influential of the Shia landholders, taking him methodically through certain evidence which had been given against him and recording his categorical denials. After he had protested vehemently that all the Hindu witnesses were in a conspiracy against him, I reminded him that upon one point he had to meet evidence given by three Mohammedan neighbours.

"They are Sunnis," he replied hotly; "in this matter the Hindus and the Sunnis are at one. The whole thing has been from the first a conspiracy between them to spoil our Moharram."

I felt instinctively that these words came from his heart. There spoke the Shia gentleman, who knew the history that lay behind the celebrations of the tenth of Moharram, and the peculiar traditions of his faith in respect of the same. Sunni Mohammedans might take out their *tazias*; they might join with enthusiasm in acclaiming the grandsons of the Prophet; it might be true that their participation was necessary to give the festival its full dignity and importance. For all that, the procession of the *Ashra* day remained to the educated Shia '*our* Moharram.' He could not feel that his Sunni brethren shared his feelings with regard to it; he was quick to suspect them of conspiring with the Hindus to mar its solemnity.

The idea of a Hindu wedding, with its heathen ritual, its music, its open display of rejoicing, being celebrated simultaneously with the procession of the *tazias* hurt the feelings of the Shia gentlemen; that the wedding procession should trespass upon the traditional route of the *tazias* seemed to them intolerable. Yet the petition presented to the Deputy Magistrate seemed to assume an inherent right to do both these things, and there had been no definite official repudiation of this attitude. It looked as if some precedent was to be established, detrimental to the due observance of their solemn festival. To minds preoccupied with uneasy suspicions, the delay in the disposal of the petition appeared to cover some sinister purpose. Could it be that it was intended to spring upon them, at the last possible moment, some intolerable order, which they would feel bound to resist to the utmost, and yet have no time in which to organise an effective resistance? If so, they must begin their preparations at once. From their point of view, the peculiar difficulty of the situation was that nothing could be done without the concurrence of the great mass of the local Mohammedans, and these were Sunnis almost to a man; an appeal must therefore be made to Moslem fanaticism generally. Moreover, the Hindu petition being in the hands of Mohammedan officials for disposal, these must in some way be discredited in the eyes of their co-religionists; the indignation of the populace must be focussed upon them personally.

I need hardly say that no evidence was ever forthcoming of what actually passed at the gatherings of influential Mohammedans, both Shias and Sunnis, in the course of the two days preceding the tenth of Moharram; but subsequent events made it clear enough that effective steps had been taken to work up Moslems of the lower orders into a mood of savage animosity, directed first against their Hindu neighbours, and secondly against the three Mohammedan officials in charge of the Moharram arrangements. The wildest rumours were afloat. The point most insisted on was that the Hindus claimed to be entitled to hold up the procession of the *tazias* while their wedding procession, with its discordant music and display of heathen rejoicing, cut into the prescribed route and proceeded along it as far as its organisers might see fit to take it. A precedent was to be established which would entitle the Hindus, for all future time, to cut the Moslem celebration to pieces at their pleasure. It was time to strike a blow for the true faith, to teach the Hindus of Amroha a lesson which would make them very chary of ever again discovering that the *Ashra* of the Mohammedans was an auspicious day for one of their heathenish festivities. As for the Deputy Magistrate and his responsible subordinates, no words were bad enough to describe their conduct. At best they were time-serving cowards, afraid to accept the responsibility of doing their plain duty by their own co-religionists; the probability was that they had been bribed.

The day of the celebration came round. The officials in charge were aware that there was a good deal of dangerous excitement abroad, but they had by this time passed orders upon the Hindu trader's petition which no fair-minded Mohammedan could deny to be reasonable and proper. They made the best arrangements they could with the police force at their disposal, and hoped for the best. The first untoward piece of news to reach them was that the procession of *tazias* had come to a dead halt. Apparently the Mohammedans were about to raise a cry that they were being prevented from conducting the celebration in their own way and in accordance with established precedents; they would, therefore, refuse to complete it, reserving the right to complain to higher authority that they had been hindered in the lawful exercise of their religion. Responsible officers hastened to the spot. They were met at first by vague and confused outcries gradually taking shape in the assertion that the men carrying the *tazias* had a perfect right to take as long as they pleased over their journey, and were not to be hustled along the route by officials anxious to find time to get a Hindu wedding procession across somewhere in the rear of theirs. This difficulty was surmounted, partly by tact and firmness on the part of the police officers, but more because those responsible for the demonstration knew in their hearts that the orders passed on the Hindu petition were unobjectionable and would afford no handle for an effective protest against the Deputy Magistrate's proceedings. Their real object in delaying the procession of *tazias* was to create trouble and to leave in the minds of the ignorant demonstrators a discontented feeling that they had somehow, after all, been hurried over the concluding portion of their route under the pressure of police interference. However, in one way or another, the procession was escorted to its customary terminus, the *tazias* were disposed of, and the Deputy Magistrate with his coadjutors returned to the house in which he had taken up his lodging.

They thought their troubles were over, but they were mistaken. From one quarter of the town after another reports came in that the Mohammedans who had followed the *tazias* were not dispersing to their homes. They were gathering in menacing groups in open spaces or in the courtyards of houses opening on to main thoroughfares. There was reason to believe that they were being harangued by fervid orators. Hindu traders were closing and barricading their shops. Something must be done to clear the streets, or at least to ascertain definitely what was afoot. Night had now fallen, and the streets of an old town like Amroha are none too well lighted. The Deputy Magistrate and his advisers collected a number of torches and organised a small party, headed by the Inspector of Police and accompanied by an armed guard of perhaps half a dozen men. Issuing forth from the house which may be conveniently spoken of as the Magistrate's lodgings, the party entered the main thoroughfare and turned to the right, northwards. They had not proceeded far before they came into collision with a sullen crowd which blocked the road in front of them and greeted the summons to disperse with shouts of abuse, followed by a shower of brickbats and an ugly rush. The Inspector was apparently taken by surprise. Either his armed police were not properly posted at the head of his column, or he hesitated to order them to open fire. Drawing his own revolver he checked the crowd for a moment by firing three shots, and then endeavoured to withdraw in good order towards the lane from which he had started. The thing was not to be done, the backward movement was in itself fatal. The crowd pressed forward, and the retreat degenerated into something very like a panic-stricken flight. Luckily the mob hesitated a moment or two at the mouth of the lane; the police officers and their party reached the gateway opening into the courtyard of the lodgings, slamming and barricading the gate behind them. So hasty and ill-organised had this movement been that in the darkness and confusion two constables of the armed guard were shut out. As they stood shouting for admission outside the barred gate, the advance-guard of the mob came pouring into the lane. The constables were Hindus, hillmen recruited from the country north of Moradabad; as they retreated down the lane someone in the mob noticed them. There was a cry of," Strike! Strike, brothers, for the faith! Begin by sacrificing these two infidels." The hillmen found themselves with their backs to the wall at the end of the blind alley and the mob advancing upon them, but they came of a fighting stock and had arms in their hands. Each slipped a cartridge into his musket and fired point-blank at their assailants, who fell hastily back to the mouth of the lane, where a furious mob was now gathering from all directions. The constables advanced a few paces, and paused irresolute. The courtyard gate was still shut and the rioters were obviously gathering for a fresh rush. At this moment a door opened in the blank wall of the lane to the right of the two men who stood gazing towards its entrance; an urgent whisper invited them to enter. It was a Hindu shopkeeper, bravely venturing incalculable risks in order to offer them a refuge in his private house. As they stepped inside, the door was hastily closed and bolted. They stood in a narrow passage leading, no doubt, to some inner courtyard, but the dim light of a lantern showed that they were at the foot of a narrow flight of stairs leading towards the roof. A tumult of voices in the lane outside appealed to the spirit of adventure now fully aroused in their breasts. Climbing the stairs they presently found themselves behind a low parapet, peering cautiously down through the darkness, with the courtyard gate of the Magistrate's lodgings only a few yards away to their right front.

Either the mob below consisted of individuals other than those who had first attacked the two constables, or its leaders took it for granted that the men had by this time been admitted into the courtyard, upon the gates of which a furious attack was now being made. Confused cries were rising, calling for crowbars or axes, or suggesting the application of fire. The blood of the two hillmen was up; there, below them, surged and clamoured the throng of their would-be murderers. They were attacking the house in which the Deputy Magistrate and the chief officers of the local police had taken refuge; their angry cries threatened the lives of the Government officials. Surely it was legitimate to defend that house by all available means? The ignorant and illiterate constables hesitated; they admitted afterwards that they had not the slightest idea whether the action they meditated would call for punishment or reward. "Surely the *Sirkar* will not hang us for saving the lives of its officers," they muttered. Anyhow, the opportunity was too tempting; they felt for their cartridge-belts and opened fire with buckshot, right down on the backs of the rioters beating upon the closed gateway. Fortunately for their opponents the two constables were anything but trained marksmen. They were firing down into the dark, and subsequent investigation showed that their shot flew wild and high. Still, the target before them was one which it was impossible altogether to miss, and nothing could have been more disconcerting to the rioters than this sudden outburst of fire on their left rear. They fled in confusion up to, and beyond, the mouth of the alley.

In the main street beyond this, however, the furious crowd of Mohammedans mustered strong. It says much for the power of fanaticism that two further attempts were made to press home the attack down the blind alley. I do not say that the same individuals returned more than once to the charge, but there were enough angry Moslems present to furnish recruits for a second, and yet a third, advance. The second was checked by the fire of the two hillmen leaning forward over the parapet of the roof, and it may be finding a steadier aim as they pointed their muskets towards the lighter background furnished by the mouth of the lane. The third attack came after a short interval; it was somewhat better organised, and by this time the mob had been joined by one or two men carrying firearms. In the interval, however, the Deputy Magistrate and the officers with him had profited by the respite. The Police Inspector had got his men in hand once more and organised the defence of the house from within. The rioters were received with shots fired from points of vantage above the threatened gateway, in addition to the flanking fire still kept up by the two hillmen from the other side of the lane. This was too much; the rioters broke in a final panic. There was nothing more to be done, and the mob melted away in all directions.

When the officials collected their forces and once more turned the corner of the blind alley into the main thoroughfare, they found themselves marching through deserted streets. In the lane itself three of the rioters lay dead; it was never ascertained what further casualties had been inflicted. Whatever dead or wounded may have been carried off in the retreat, all were carefully concealed or disposed of in secret. In one of the main streets, however, a considerable distance from the scene of the actual fighting, one man lay dead by the roadside in front of a closed shop. It was an unfortunate Hindu, his skull beaten in by blows, presumably inflicted by the quarter-staff of bamboo, the ordinary fighting weapon of the Indian peasant. There was consequently a charge of murder committed in the course of a riot amongst the counts in the indictment, upon which twenty-nine Mohammedans of Amroha eventually appeared before my court for trial.

The story of this trial, in many respects the most interesting and important one over which it fell to my lot to preside as a Sessions Judge, can scarcely be told in any detail, so as to make it interesting to English readers. It lasted just eight weeks. At first I made the mistake of trying to handle this formidable addition to my cause list by prolonging the sittings of the court beyond the usual hours. This served no good purpose: judicial work is not to be done efficiently under pressure of time, least of all in the poisonous heat of June, July, and August, in the plains of India. Moreover, I came to realise that I was throwing an intolerable burden on the learned counsel engaged in the case. We have no order of solicitors in India, away from the Presidency towns; much of the work which would have been done by solicitors in England had perforce to be done by counsel, whether for the prosecution or for the defence, in the intervals between the sittings of the court. We actually made better progress when I consented to ease off the pressure and appealed to the co-operation of the bar to concentrate on the essentials of the case.

These were in the main three. I had to ascertain the broad facts which I have already laid before the reader, determining more particularly whether any ill-considered action on the part of the authorities could fairly be blamed for the disastrous issue. Next came the question of the murder of the unfortunate Hindu. Finally, I had to sum up, as against each individual accused, the evidence implicating him personally in whatever offence against the law had been committed. The accused included only three or four of the leading Shia gentry; the great majority were Sunnis of the lower orders. On the main issue the defence never got much nearer to setting up a case of their own than the contention that the Mohammedans would have dispersed quietly to their homes if they had been left alone after the procession of the *tazias* was over, or at any rate that there must have been something needlessly provocative about the action of the police party which set out, by torch-light, to clear the streets. Here the evidence left no doubt in my mind that there was serious mischief afoot, and that inaction on the part of the police would have resulted in a more dangerous, because more methodical and better organised, outbreak of disorder in the course of the night.

The murder charge broke down ; there was no evidence forthcoming on which the court could hold any of the accused accountable for the death of the unfortunate Hindu. He proved to be an entirely inoffensive person, quite unconnected with the petitioner whose wedding procession had been the starting-point of the trouble. It could not be shown that he was personally obnoxious, or even previously known, to any of the accused men. Years afterwards, in connection with a riot in which the Hindus of a large city had risen against their Mohammedan neighbours, I came across definite evidence of the manner in which an excited mob will set upon, and beat the life out of, some ill-starred individual who simply happens to blunder across their path. Something of the sort must have occurred at Amroha, but I came to the conclusion that the crime had been witnessed by no one except the actual perpetrators. One man said he had seen it ; and a lurid account he gave of the business, putting one of the principal Shia accused forward as the chief murderer. As a matter of fact, the thing most against this particular accused proved to be his own defence. This was an *alibi* which, when carefully sifted, amounted to something very like proof that he had hastily left Amroha by the first available train after the riot was over, and had proceeded to concoct false evidence to prove that he had done so two days previously. What saved him was the conclusive breakdown of the prosecution witness under a searching cross-examination. He was certainly a very queer person. To begin with, he was not really a resident of the town of Amroha; he lived in quarters near the railway station, more than a mile distant. As for his presence in the town on the night in question, if he had elected to say that he had simply wandered down there, for no particular reason beyond the fact that he was bored with his own company in the railway lines, I should probably have believed him, and he certainly could not have been contradicted. He preferred to tell a long story, which grew more and more incredible as his cross-examination proceeded. If he had really been where he said he was at the time of the murder, and had seen what he said he saw, it was as nearly certain as anything can be which depends on the probable action of human beings under given circumstances, that the police would have found two corpses lying by the side of the deserted road instead of only one. When I came to my final review of the entire evidence, gathering together loose threads and scattered hints, I came to a conclusion about him which I have other reasons for believing was not far from the truth. The man had, in fact, come into the town of Amroha "about lamp-lighting time," as the Indians say. The object of his visit, which he was doggedly determined not to disclose, had been to meet a light-of-love at her rooms in one of the main serais. This serai had been raided by a section of the mob, whether out of mere whim, or on the suggestion of some Puritanically-minded Shia, it is impossible to say. The witness had just escaped with his life from a hot pursuit. Precisely why this adventure had resulted in his coming forward with a story which, if believed, would have sent one of the leading Shias to the gallows I could never learn.

When it came to sifting out the evidence against individual accused I had an anxious task before me. My assessors gave me little assistance; the impression they left on my mind was that nothing would have induced them to find any of the accused guilty of murder; but that if it was a mere question of punishing a certain number of the accused for minor offences of rioting and conspiracy, it really could not matter very much which of them the court might choose to select for punishment. One little group of witnesses I found it particularly hard to deal with. At a somewhat late stage of the trial three witnesses came forward who had a very curious story to tell. They were Sunni Mohammedans of what one might call the lower middle class. They lived in two houses situated between what I have spoken of as the Deputy Magistrate's lodgings and the main thoroughfare into which the blind alley opened. In substance their story was that, late in the evening of the *Ashra*, but before any disturbance had actually broken out, they had been approached by two or three of the leading Shias, who asked them in so many words whether they would be prepared to admit into their houses men desirous of making an attack upon the aforesaid lodgings. They replied in the negative, and took care to close their house doors; no attempt was made to force them.

If I had accepted this evidence I should have convicted, upon charges of conspiracy and abetment of rioting, two leading gentlemen whom I finally acquitted on the ground that their complicity in the affair was not satisfactorily proved. I heard afterwards that, when the appeals from my decision were argued before the High Court at Allahabad, two learned Judges of that Court stated openly that, if I had seen fit to accept the evidence of the three Sunnis, they could have given no reason for my not doing so. This was just the kind of point which one would greatly prefer to leave to the determination of an honest and intelligent jury. As the foreman of such a jury, I should have turned to my fellows with some such remark as, "Now, what about those three Mohammedan witnesses? If you want to know my opinion, I did not believe a word they said; but how did they strike you?" If the impression produced by this testimony on the minds of the other jurymen had been the same, we should just have shrugged our shoulders and passed on to something else. Our disbelief would have been embodied in our verdict, but no one could have called upon us to formulate precise reasons for it; indeed, we might not necessarily have all been influenced by identical reasons. On the other hand, it is conceivable that the evidence of the three men had produced quite a different effect upon minds just as capable and intelligent as my own: the mere knowledge that this was so would have given me food for thought. I might have been brought, not merely to reconsider, but to reverse my original opinion. That is the advantage of the jury system; it tends to eliminate the personal equation; it gives solidity and confidence to the concurrent workings of twelve honest minds. As matters stood, I could only give effect to a disbelief for which I found it desperately difficult to assign specific reasons. The story told by the witnesses was a queer one, but obviously there was a great deal the court did not know about the events of that day, and the story of the riot itself contained curious and surprising features. What I was really up against was the question—why should the witnesses have come forward with this story if it was not true? I think I can answer this question more frankly now than I could do when called upon to deliver a considered judgment, based upon the recorded evidence, and upon nothing else. I do not say that the theory I formed respecting the evidence of these three witnesses was necessarily correct, but I give it for what it is worth. I do know as a fact that, after the riot was over and the Moslem community of Amroha was counting up its losses and speculating as to what might yet have to be endured in the way of punishment, there was considerable recrimination between Sunnis and Shias. As to the exact nature of those recriminations I have very little to go upon, but I am gravely mistaken if they did not take some such form as this. The Shias remained obstinately suspicious that there had been a conspiracy to provoke them into an attitude of opposition to established authority, and then leave them in the lurch by passing orders on the Hindu petition which were in fact unobjectionable. They believed that the leading Sunnis had previous information of the orders intended to be passed, and could have got the crowds to go quietly home after the procession was over, if they had frankly used their influence to that end. The Sunnis not merely denied all this, but retorted with the charge that the Shia gentry had first stirred the fanaticism of the masses beyond possibility of restraint, and had then retired discreetly into the background, leaving their wretched dupes to be shot down first and the survivors brought up for punishment afterwards. My suspicion, therefore, was, and remains, that the three Sunni witnesses were embroidering upon an incident which did in fact occur, under quite different circumstances and much later in the day, the object of their embroidery being that two at any rate of the Shia gentry should share any punishments that might be going.

In the end only one of the leading Shias was included in the list of the accused whom I found guilty on the charges of rioting and conspiracy. The name of another, a hot-headed youngster, had cropped up more than once in the evidence given before me, but the police had failed to find him. He was arrested later, and convicted and sentenced by a Magistrate. The majority of the accused whom I convicted were Sunnis of the lower orders. I felt sorry for the poor wretches, and believed that the lesson taught by the muskets of the two little hillmen was almost a sufficient deterrent for the future. The leniency of the sentences I passed excited some comment, but the learned Judges of the Allahabad High Court, in dismissing all the appeals against my decision, merely remarked that as regards the sentences passed they " found nothing to criticise."

IV.

TWO CHEVALIERS D'INDUSTRIE.

I SUPPOSE that a Judge's work, all the world over, tends towards monotony; it certainly does so in India. The professional criminal mostly makes his living by some form of house-breaking or highway robbery; it is a mere variant on the theme when the numbers engaged in one or other of these offences raise the crime to the dignity of a 'dacoity.' Of the homicides which come before one for trial, a large proportion are committed in the course of faction fights, sometimes arising out of religious differences but more frequently from the land hunger of the Indian peasant. Add to these the inevitable percentage of murders traceable to the motive of sex, and a sprinkling of characteristically Indian crimes such as cattle-lifting, cattle-poisoning, and the kidnapping of marriageable girls, and you pretty well exhaust the list of cases likely to appear on the ordinary calendar of a Sessions Judge in Northern India. This must be the reason why I find myself dwelling with something like fondness on my recollections of two criminals who displayed definite originality in their methods. Each of them was something of a genius in his particular line, and in both cases it was a curious accident which caught the offender in the meshes of the criminal law.

As regards Sheikh Miran, indeed, apart from the general outlines of his career, what chiefly remains in my memory is that he owed his conviction, in the first instance, to the testimony afforded by the operations of an insignificant insect, a tiny worm which seeks its humble livelihood wherever there are accumulations of paper to be found. The man was a professional forger of amazing skill and resourcefulness. The mere ability to imitate a particular handwriting was the smallest part of his equipment. He had perfected a duplicating apparatus which enabled him to reproduce, not merely with accuracy, but with the most convincing verisimilitude, the impress of an ancient seal or stamp. He could write the fluent Persian employed in legal documents and royal grants, in days long anterior to the British annexation of Oudh, with a fidelity to the general style of such compositions and the script of ancient times, which fairly baffled expert examination. When the police raided his little workshop, tucked away in a quiet corner of Lucknow, they found that he possessed a regular stock of the kind of paper used in ancient documents, such as *firmans* of the Court of Delhi or grants of land made by the Kings of Oudh. He had also contrived to acquire, in spite of all official regulations intended to preclude the possibility of such accumulations, a small stock of blank stamped papers.

As regards the details of the particular case which brought Sheikh Miran to the dock of the Sessions Judge's Court, I have kept no memoranda, but I have a clear enough recollection of the essentials. A suit was pending in the Civil Court regarding the right of succession to a certain estate. In the Oudh Laws Act it is expressly laid down that our Courts will administer the civil law of the parties, whether Hindus or Mohammedans, as modified by family or tribal customs. The essential issue in this particular case was whether the right of succession was or was not governed by a family custom. At a certain stage of the inquiry a petition was presented on behalf of one of the parties, asking that search be made in the Record Room of the District Judge of Lucknow. The petitioner represented that many years ago, in fact, shortly after the annexation of Oudh, there had been a dispute in his family, which had come before the Commissioner of Lucknow, then the highest court of civil jurisdiction; if the record of that litigation could be discovered, it was believed that it would throw some light on the question now in dispute. Search was duly made, and the next application from the same litigant was that the court would be pleased to call for and inspect a particular record, duly described according to its serial number and the date of its decision. The file was disinterred from the recesses of the Record Room and laid before the Subordinate Judge. The process of years and the operation of the elaborate rules for the weeding-out of papers the preservation of which ceases to be essential after the lapse of a specified time, had cut it down to the barest skeleton. It did, however, contain a judgment in the vernacular, stamped with the seal of the court and bearing the English signature of the Commissioner, showing that the title of an ancestor of the parties to the pending litigation had at that time been challenged, and deciding the matter in his favour. This in itself had no bearing on the point now in dispute, but the judgment took note of the fact that the decision rested largely upon an ancient *firman*, or grant, issued from the Imperial Court at Delhi in favour of an ancestor of the gentleman concerned. And the next paper on the record was the *firman* itself: the paper on which it was written, its penmanship, its language and the impress it purported to bear of an ancient seal all appeared absolutely convincing. It contained a clause to the effect that the property covered by the grant would descend to the heirs of the grantee according to a special rule of inheritance, which was precisely the rule contended for by the party to the pending litigation who had been fortunate enough to discover this invaluable piece of evidence, hidden away in a remote corner of the public Record Room. It need hardly be said that the lawyers on the other side subjected the papers to the minutest scrutiny. The important point obviously was the reference to the *firman* in the ancient judgment of the Commissioner of Lucknow. On the face of it this seemed to prove that the *firman* had, in fact, been produced in that court by a descendant of the grantee and had lain for over half a century in the safe custody of the Record Room; it furnished solid ground for a presumption of genuineness in favour of that document. The lawyers turned to the flimsy page on which the judgment was engrossed, and concentrated their attention on the two vital points, the signature and the seal of the court. There was something odd about the signature; it was an illegible scrawl which no one could read as representing any particular English surname, whether with or without the initials prefixed. It was certainly open to the suggestion that the badly written signature of an English officer, whose name was not, in fact, known to the persons concerned, had been imitated by a forger imperfectly acquainted with the English language or script, however skilful he might be in writing the vernacular. This, however, could only be a suggestion, open to a counter-argument too obvious to require stating. There remained the seal of the Court, and, of course, the first question was whether this was in fact the seal used by the Civil Court of highest jurisdiction in Lucknow at the date of the judgment. The Subordinate Judge, upon application duly made, called for the entire bundle of records from which this particular one had been extracted. It was a thin bundle, containing two or three other records at most. An examination of these showed that a seal giving a similar impress to that on the disputed judgment was, in fact, in use at that time; but it brought to light another circumstance which proved conclusively that a forgery had been committed, as skilful as it was daring. A minute boring worm had been at work in the bundle of old records—the traces of its operations were here and there and everywhere. In particular, that part of the paper which bore the impress of the Court's seal, in the very next record to the one containing the *firman*, showed four or five small holes, irregularly distributed over its surface. In the disputed judgment the paper was nowhere perforated, but the impress of the seal showed four or five spots of yellowish-white, where the ink of the seal had not reached the paper. One impression was carefully superimposed on the other, and the witness of the worm sufficed to declare the truth. Precisely in those places where the genuine impress had been perforated, there and nowhere else did the blank spots appear upon the forgery.

Obviously both the records, or more probably the whole of the small bundle containing the two files, had been temporarily abstracted from the Record Room. They had been in the hands of a forger possessed of an apparatus enabling him to construct an efficient seal from the impress of one upon any old paper. He had thus been able to reproduce an all too faithful replica of the genuine impress on the counterfeit which was to be substituted for the record of the judgment delivered many years before in an ancient litigation. As the object of the substitution could only be to provide official attestation of the genuineness of the *firman*, the forger must be a person capable of producing an imitation of an ancient grant of the Delhi Court so complete in every respect as to challenge contradiction. He had probably done his work under considerable pressure of time. The abstraction of papers from the Record Room, whether with or without the connivance of a subordinate member of the staff, is not an impossibility; but it is a risky business, and the persons concerned would not desire the papers to remain absent an hour longer than was absolutely necessary. This is the best reason I can suggest for the failure to notice the tell-tale spots left in the forged impression by the fact that the counterfeit seal had missed contact with the paper upon which it was modelled, wherever that paper had been eaten through.

As it happened, the chances of official life called me away from Lucknow while the investigation into these matters was still pending. I had nothing to do with the proceedings against Sheikh Miran which followed upon my departure. To the best of my recollection, the police raid upon his workshop was due to nothing more romantic than information supplied by some panic-stricken accomplice. The discoveries there made furnished material for more than one prosecution. What I learnt regarding the man's powers, and the scale on which he had apparently been conducting his operations, left me wondering whether the investigation would result in the discovery of cases in which his forgeries had successfully imposed upon the courts of law, but so far as I know this was never proved. The man himself, I was told, dropped some dark hints concerning revelations he might make if he were driven too far, but either this was mere bluff or he decided to keep faith with those who had employed him. The last I heard of him was a not wholly unreasonable plea on his part that, whatever he might have done, the interests of justice could not require that successive prosecutions and cumulative sentences should shut him up in prison for the rest of his life.

Artist as Miran undoubtedly was in his own particular line, he was something of a specialist. He lacked the versatility and resourcefulness, the impish delight in his own experiments on human credulity, the *gout de mensonge artistique* which I found so attractive in the man whom I knew as Parmatma Sahai. I remember thinking at the time that, if I could only induce this adventurer to give me a detailed account of his career up to date, I might well produce a book worthy to take its place as a classic beside Meadows Taylor's 'Autobiography of a Thug.' For reasons which the discerning reader will appreciate, I prefer to tell the following story under the decent veil of imaginary names of persons and places, except for the name 'Parmatma Sahai,' which was itself a pseudonym the very coinage of which was a characteristic touch of its creator's art.

My story opens with the Rev. Stephen Podmore sitting in the back verandah of his little house, looking out upon the Mission compound at Rasulabad. The lamp had just been lighted in the room behind him ; but it was cooler outside, and the worthy Padre sat on for a time, resting his body and revolving in his mind certain aspects of his work. He was just back from a tour round the villages in which lived his scattered converts. His camping equipment was of the simplest : a single bullock-cart, with a lad to drive the sturdy pair of bullocks, carried the missionary, his one attendant and factotum, and all the baggage requisite for a ten days' journey. The cart itself was readily convertible into a sleeping-tent. He made a point of taking little with him in the way of provisions, relying on such food as could be purchased in any village and seeking, so far as the requirements of health permitted, to assimilate his way of life to that of his humble converts. Humble they certainly were, the enormous majority of them drawn from amongst the 'untouchables,' the outcasts of Hindu society. In this direction, undoubtedly, the prospect opened out. Down at the very bottom of its complex structure the pyramid of Hinduism was unstable ; a movement towards social emancipation was stirring amongst the dumb masses, no longer content to be, like their forefathers, something worse than hewers of wood and drawers of water to the classes above them. Not long ago Mr Podmore had been asked, by an English official, what sort of Christians he thought he was making out of the densely ignorant outcasts who were coming to him for baptism. At the time he had been content to reply that he was less concerned with the present generation of converts than with their children whom he was passing through his Mission schools, but the question recurred to him and started a train of thought. His features relaxed into a smile as he called to mind an incident of his recent tour. He had gone considerably out of his way to visit one of these recent converts at his own village. As he approached the doorway of the thatched hut he found, as he had fully expected to find, that it differed in no way from those around it. Door-posts and lintel bore the traditional, immemorial signs; there was the ancient charm against the wrath of the Goddess of Smallpox, and there the emblem which barred the humble threshold to the entrance of poisonous snakes. In the presence of the gathering crowd of interested neighbours he had exhorted the new-made Christian to have the courage of his faith. "You are now under the protection of Jesus, the Messiah; why should you grieve Him by even pretending to appeal to the demons you worshipped in your ignorance?" And under the eyes of his awe-struck neighbours the master of the house had erased and destroyed and cleansed, until his teacher could enter, with the prayer of the earliest missionaries—"Peace be to this house!" Not many weeks ago the man would have been appalled at the very notion of such a sacrilege. The critics might say what they pleased, but the Gospel did come as a ray of light into dense darkness; it did bring with it a loosening of ancient fetters, an uplift which was not wholly material.

And yet—what was to be the outcome of it all? Suppose this movement, of which he could sense the first stirrings, were to gather momentum? Could the various missionary societies cope with a real 'mass movement' of the pariahs and outcasts of India towards Christianity? And what of the high-caste Hindus? Already this growing extension of missionary labour in the direction of the 'untouchables' was rousing them from their attitude of contemptuous toleration. It was making it increasingly difficult to maintain any sort of contact with the upper strata of Hinduism. Years ago, Christian missionaries had sought to acquire a hold upon them through the medium of English education; the effort had not proved much of a success, and opportunities for pursuing it further were diminishing every year. Meanwhile, a class of educated Hindus had grown up who were far more definitely antagonistic to Christianity than their fathers had ever been. One could only be patient and alert for every opportunity chance might offer of establishing friendly relations.

I like to think that it was at some such stage in his meditations that the good Padre was interrupted by a message that a man was outside, urgently demanding to see him. The visitor gave his name as Parmatma Sahai, obviously a *brahman* and very possibly a religious leader in his community. When ushered into the little sitting-room, a stockily built man of middle age, with melancholy eyes and a gentle voice, he began with many apologies for his intrusion. He had an appeal to make on behalf of one in desperate need of help. Of course, he himself was not a Christian ; if he might venture to say so, he was earnestly devoted to the faith of his ancestors, and sought to order his life according to its precepts. Yet he had heard much of the wide charity of Christian missionaries, of their doctrine of universal brotherhood, which recognised no limitations of caste or creed. It was to this that he ventured to appeal. Encouraged to proceed, he said that he had come on behalf of a friend.

" I might say that he is the best friend, perhaps the only friend, I have in the world. He is a young man, or at anyrate, in the prime of life ; he is suffering from no disease—yet he will never see the light of another day. Yes, you have rightly divined my meaning ; he is irrevocably resolved upon taking his own life. I have argued out the question with him long and earnestly. We have discussed it from the religious point of view. Of course, we Hindus, with our belief in reincarnation, do not look upon suicide quite in the same light as Christians do ; but I am, indeed, persuaded that a man who takes it upon himself to fix the termination of his present stage of existence must expiate this act by suffering, it may be by some degradation, in the next. What of that? A man may be so persecuted by fate, so hemmed in by misfortunes, that he must needs accept the only way of escape open to him. At least, this is my friend's feeling; his purpose is fixed. I said I had come to make an appeal on his behalf; this is both true and untrue. My appeal is on behalf of one whom he loves better than himself—his young wife whose love for him has been the ruin of her life, and in a sense of his own, also."

The visitor was overcome with emotion. Brokenly, and with many protests that it was impossible for him to enter into precise details, he unfolded his pitiful story. His friend had been brought up to be a Pandit, a priest and teacher of the Hindu religion. His wife had been taken from a priestly family, residents of the sacred city of Mathura, and intensely proud of their religious status. Now, his friend had come by degrees to interest himself more and more in the cure of bodies rather than of souls. He had studied deeply the Hindu system of medicine. With the progress of these studies he had come to feel an invincible distaste for some of the methods by which men of the priestly class earned their livelihood. However pure and enlightened might be their private views on God and religion, it could not be denied that they traded upon the superstitions of the vulgar; they countenanced, they encouraged a gross idolatry in which they did not themselves believe. His friend had determined to devote himself entirely to the practice of medicine; this resolution, and certain expressions which he had rashly let fall when debating the matter with members of his wife's family, had led to a bitter feud between them. They had retaliated by taking his wife from him, but her love for him was such that she had contrived to escape from the custody in which they endeavoured to keep her. He had, in fact, eloped with his own wife; they had left Mathura together. He had tried to set up as a medical practitioner at Delhi, but the malignant persecution of his wife's relatives had followed him there. By persistent slanders, by invoking against him the tremendous machinery of the caste organisation, they had made it impossible for him to earn his living. There were complications into which he could not enter; his wife had claims against her own family, not merely for jewelry, but for landed property which they were wrongfully keeping from her. He had reason to fear a fresh attempt to kidnap her from him. They had fled from Delhi in a state of utter destitution. His friend might have endured sheer starvation for himself with fortitude, but it was terrible to be no longer able to provide her with the common necessaries of life. He honestly believed that it would be better for her if he were no longer in this world. If he could find for her an asylum in which she could be sure of protection, where she would be treated with the compassion due to her unmerited misfortunes, his own death would in the long-run prove the best thing possible for her. Her own family would relent, and she would be in a position to make terms with them. In short, the request he had to make was that this unhappy lady, so soon to be a widow, might be received into the safe shelter of the Mission house. He was sure that she would be treated with the consideration she deserved. In no long time, when the news of her husband's death and of her whereabouts reached her family, they would be certain to communicate with the missionaries. They would be anxious to avoid scandal, ready to offer reasonable terms. All he asked was a safe asylum for her, and a solemn promise that she would not be delivered up to anyone except with her free consent.

The intelligent reader will already have anticipated the main outlines of the conversation that followed. From every conceivable point of view the story told by his visitor was calculated to arouse the sympathetic interest of the good Padre. Noting the obvious emotion displayed by the narrator, and reading between the lines of his narration, his hearer could scarcely avoid drawing a certain inference. With kindly urgency he pressed for perfect frankness, and extracted the avowal he felt certain must follow. Yes, Parmatma Sahai admitted, it was wrong for him to appeal for help unless he was prepared to confess all; besides, it was clearly useless to attempt to deceive so shrewd a listener. It was true; he was himself his own friend, the poor wretch whose sad story he had unveiled. It was his own wife for whom he was appealing. Still, the essential facts remained as he had stated them; his own resolution was irrevocably fixed. All he asked was that he might be permitted to leave this life with his mind freed from anxiety on her account. With a shrewd grasp of the situation as it appeared to him, Mr Podmore began to raise difficulties as to the immediate granting of the request. Time was needed to prepare suitable accommodation for the proposed guest. Would not her husband bring her on the following morning?

His visitor smiled sadly. "You must allow me, sir," he remarked, "the perspicacity to see through your innocent artifice as readily as you discerned the less excusable falsehood with which I embellished my otherwise truthful narrative. You would induce me at least to postpone the execution of my purpose; you think that a night's rest may bring a change of mind. I know that you are mistaken; I must leave you under no illusion on this point. Yet it is a matter of complete indifference to me whether I terminate this stage of my unhappy existence a few hours earlier or a few hours later. My difficulty lies elsewhere. With all your kindness, you have not grasped the full urgency of the situation. I blush to say it, but she has tasted no food to-day."

It is scarcely necessary to add that the Mission House opened its hospitable portals that very night to its strange guest. The only condition imposed was that Parmatma Sahai himself should consent to share the hospitality; a quiet corner would be found somewhere for him to repose in. The ladies in charge of the *zenana* quarters would look after his wife. The question of his future might be left open for further discussion the following day. When the time for this came, the missionary slowly extorted from his reluctant auditor the admission that it would not be right for the latter to take his own life, so long as the faintest hope remained that he might yet find useful and honourable employment for his days. Inevitably, this led to a discussion of ways and means. It appeared that Parmatma Sahai, in his hasty flight from Delhi, had consigned two large boxes to the care of the railway company. The purchase of third-class tickets for his wife and himself had drained him of his last coppers: the luggage had been consigned—as we say in India, 'bearing'—the freight to be paid on delivery. This led up to the first cash transaction between the parties. It was with fifty rupees in his pocket that Parmatma Sahai left for the railway station to rescue his baggage, and thereafter to find for himself humble lodgings in which he might settle down to the career of a Hindu physician in Rasulabad.

The story of the weeks that followed was never laid before me in full detail. The lady remained on as an honoured guest in the Mission *zenana*. From what I subsequently learnt concerning her previous history, I was left wondering whether her eventual departure was not followed by some sort of moral fumigation or disinfection of those hospitable quarters. Parmatma Sahai visited her frequently; he made himself a *persona grata* with the entire community. It was not long before he had drawn on Mr Podmore for another small advance in cash; but I always believed that he valued even more the tribute to his powers involved in the fact that one of the maiden ladies working in the Mission presented him with a handsome little gold watch, to help him to maintain that punctuality in the keeping of appointments which is so necessary to a physician with a growing practice. This was the position his friends at the Mission steadfastly believed him to occupy.

What he was really doing in Rasulabad, apart from his visits to the Mission and his frequent and intimate conversations with the Rev. Stephen Podmore, I never learnt. That he did gain admission into quite respectable Hindu society I infer from one little episode which came to my knowledge some time after my personal acquaintance with the man had finally terminated. It is worth setting down as an illustration of Parmatma Sahai's fertility of resource. A good friend of mine in Rasulabad was a Deputy Magistrate who was really a Pandit, a *brahman* of the highest caste. He met the supposed physician at the house of a friend, and something about the man's appearance or conversation made him vaguely suspicious. Contriving to draw him aside, he addressed a remark to him in the Sanskrit language. Parmatma Sahai did not know two words of Sanskrit, but he parried the thrust on the instant. "Ah, brother," he exclaimed, "nothing could afford me greater pleasure than a conversation in that noble tongue, especially with one who speaks it with such purity and elegance. Alas! I am under a vow that forbids me, for a period of one year, to use that sacred language except in my devotions. The year has only two months to run now, so the pleasure is but deferred." Nor was this all. The man was astute enough to provide even against the possibility that this ingenious explanation might not be wholly believed. Without committing himself to any positive assertion that could be brought up against him afterwards, he contrived to leave the worthy Deputy Magistrate with an uneasy suspicion that he had come across an agent of the Secret Service, and might seriously embarrass some critical investigation if he were to press his inquiries too far.

With all the opportunities I afterwards enjoyed for sifting the matter, I never quite understood how Parmatma Sahai brought off his final coup. Obviously, he had won the complete confidence of the Rev. Stephen Podmore; in that quarter, to use an Americanism, what he said went. I think also that, in some not very definite fashion, his friendship was regarded as valuable. Perhaps it offered to the missionary possibilities of friendly intercourse with a section of Hindu society otherwise out of his reach. At anyrate, a day came when Parmatma Sahai confided to him that he only required a little capital in order to avail himself of an opportunity of permanently establishing himself in Rasulabad. Whether the money was to be paid for the purchase of a practice, as we should understand the transaction in England, I am not quite clear. The certain thing was that, if Parmatma Sahai could only raise the necessary money at once on reasonable terms, he would be able to take a house and settle down, with the prospect of earning an income which would make the speedy repayment of the loan an easy matter. His arguments proved convincing. Mr Podmore got out his cheque book, and Parmatma Sahai was able to draw from the local banker a sum of six hundred rupees in currency notes and cash. He left as security a promissory note, the signature 'Parmatma Sahai' in English letters sprawling gleefully across the stamp which gave the document legal validity; it was a promise to pay the Rev. S. Podmore on demand the sum of six hundred rupees 'for value received.'

By what was unquestionably something more than a coincidence, Mr Podmore was due to leave Rasulabad that night to attend a Missionary Conference which would detain him for about a week. The following morning Parmatma Sahai presented himself at the Mission House to take away his wife. He expressed surprise that the good ladies there knew nothing of his intention, made some mild joke regarding the worthy Padre's intense preoccupation with the problems under discussion at the pending Conference, which must, he supposed, have prevented him from mentioning a matter that had been fully settled the previous afternoon, escorted his wife and her few belongings into a hired conveyance, and so vanished for a time out of the ken of the good missionaries of Rasulabad. The weeks grew into months, but no news reached them of the learned physician; their solitary memento of him, the promissory note, remained locked away in the Mission safe.

As to the circumstances which led to the renewal of the interrupted acquaintance, I must warn the reader that I never learnt more than the barest outline; the account which follows is, however, accurate enough in essentials. A long day's journey by train from Rasulabad lies the busy manufacturing town and mart of Kampur. At one of the principal serais of this place there arrived, some months after the disappearance of Parmatma Sahai, an individual—I believe he called himself by a Mohammedan name—whose movements were characterised by a sort of ostentatious secrecy. It was whispered about the place that he was a confidential agent of the Criminal Investigation Department; it was certainly in this capacity that he visited, first the head of an important Christian organisation in Kampur, and later the principal leader of the Arya Samaj. This latter is a society about which I can only say that I wish I knew a great deal more than I do. It stands for progressive and militant Hinduism. On the one hand, its leaders are often at odds with orthodox Brahmanism on questions of social reform; on the other, they carry on an active counter-propaganda, directed both against Christian Missions and the religious beliefs of their Moslem fellow-countrymen. To the head of each of these organisations his mysterious visitor had much to say, and much more to insinuate, against the other. Not only was he collecting information which might be expected to result in a sensational prosecution, but he was in a position to supply each of his auditors with quite startling information regarding underhand, and even criminal, activities on the part of the other. In each place he was heard with close attention, his promises to prosecute his inquiries were noted, and an appointment was made for a further visit. The truth was that he had unwittingly fallen into a snare laid for him by the mere existence of a fact, not merely outside his knowledge, but probably beyond the range of his imagination. Apart from what I may, with all respect, describe as their professional activities, the Christian missionary and the Arya Samajist were excellent friends. Each had learnt to know the other, and to entertain for him feelings of sincere respect, which made the dark tales and darker insinuations of the mysterious visitor frankly incredible to them both.

The two men came together, each desirous only to inform the other that there was some extraordinary plot afoot. They compared notes, decided that they had to deal with a really dangerous criminal, played with their man just sufficiently to make sure that he had furnished them with adequate materials for a prosecution, and then handed him over to the police. I do not know what the precise charge was, but the District Magistrate of Kampur took up the case and found that the offence committed could be adequately dealt with by his own court. I believe the sentence he passed went to the full limit of his powers, rigorous imprisonment for two years.

Some account of this very interesting prosecution got into the public press, and it may be that further details appeared in some periodical dealing exclusively with matters of interest to Christian missionaries. At anyrate, the facts came under discussion in the Mission House at Rasulabad. Beyond doubt the proceedings of this adventurer at Kampur bore a certain family likeness to those of their vanished acquaintance, Parmatma Sahai. The Rev. Stephen Podmore made certain inquiries by letter, followed them up by a journey to Kampur, and ran his man to earth in the local jail. The ultimate result was the appearance of Parmatma Sahai, *alias* one or two other things, before me as Sessions Judge of Rasulabad, to answer sundry charges framed under the chapter of the Indian Penal Code which deals with the offence of 'cheating' and its various aggravations.

The trial was an extraordinary one. I do not know that I ever presided over one at all like it. The accused was obviously enjoying himself for every minute of the four or five solid days over which he contrived to protract it. He conducted his own defence, and I allowed him the full latitude one feels bound to give an accused who has been unable to secure proper legal assistance. Not that he needed any. His whole defence was a masterpiece of cool impudence which no lawyer could have attempted to rival. Moreover, the man knew well enough that he was in for another period in jail, but thought he could at least make the process of securing his conviction as unpleasant as possible for everyone concerned. He kept the unfortunate Mr Podmore under cross-examination for something like a day and a half. He called for the cheque-book in which the cheque for six hundred rupees had been written, and demanded full particulars about the entry on every single counterfoil. His point was that this alleged loan had either been made from the general funds of the Mission, or out of Mr Podmore's private resources. The former, he would contend, was clearly impossible, because it would amount to malversation to apply Mission funds to any such purpose. If the latter were alleged, then he called upon the prosecutor to explain how he had managed to accumulate such a sum out of his slender stipend. When the Mission lady came into the witness-box to depose respecting the small matter of the gold watch, I had to interfere to check the insolence with which the prisoner endeavoured to treat her. He revenged himself later by pouring out a perfect flood of sly innuendo and direct slander. In his final address to the Court he had the impudence to contend that her evidence was entitled to no credit, because the English Joint

Magistrate who conducted the preliminary investigation had not merely accommodated her with a seat in his court (which was probably true enough), but had been holding her hand under the table the whole time that she was under examination.

One characteristic episode occurred outside the court, on the morning on which Mr Podmore attended for the second part of his cross-examination. The accused, being already a convict on the Kampur charge, was in the custody of two constables. It was a hot morning, and they had their man sitting outside the court-house, in the shade of a tree near the witness-shed. The dear old missionary was ill-advised enough to go up and speak to him.

"Come, Parmatma Sahai," he said, "you must feel in your heart that you have treated me very badly. How can you have the conscience to persist in your wicked assertion that I forged your promissory note? I appeal to your better feelings to make a clean breast of the matter, and I will myself appeal to the Judge to deal leniently with you."

The accused answered with some ribald jest, and the old gentleman was walking sadly away when a voice called after him.

"Mr Podmore! Mr Podmore!"

He stopped and turned round, an interested crowd of onlookers having by this time collected. "I only wanted to ask," said Parmatma Sahai, "do you *still* pray for me?"

The rascal gave me all the trouble he could in the matter of summoning witnesses for the defence. If he could have had his way, a score or so of respectable gentlemen, officials and others, would have been hauled up from every part of Northern India to depose to his excellent character. I firmly insisted that he must first deposit money for their expenses, which he declared himself wholly unable to do. One substantial banker and landholder I allowed him to call away from his work in a fairly distant part of the province, whose evidence afforded me at least the satisfaction of pointing out to the accused that, if this was a sample of what his witnesses to character had to say, it was just as well for him that I had left the remainder undisturbed.

The case was not without its legal pitfalls. The Joint Magistrate had framed the charge in the form that the accused, being in fact a Mohammedan, had deceived the Rev. Stephen Podmore into believing him to be a high-caste Hindu, and had thereby induced him to deliver valuable property. This would not do at all. To begin with, though I believe the man was really a Mohammedan, the prosecution had not proved the fact. In the second place, the good missionary was not prepared to admit that his charity towards the accused had been determined by considerations of caste or race. Of course, the whole story whereby his sympathies had been enlisted was a preposterous romance ; but as regards the six hundred rupees, at anyrate, the essence of the swindle lay in the fact that the accused had obtained them on a promise of repayment which he never had the faintest intention of honouring, even in the improbable event of his being in a position to do so. His intentions in the matter were abundantly established by the circumstantial evidence. The Criminal Procedure Code provides for the amendment of the charge, when necessary, by the Sessions Judge, and I exercised that power. To the substantial term of imprisonment which I imposed, I added a fine of one hundred rupees, with direction that the money, if realised, should be paid as partial compensation to the defrauded missionary. I had but faint hopes in this matter, and they came to nothing, but my efforts to collect the fine led to my learning a little more about the man's past career.

I addressed myself, in the first instance, to the District Magistrate of Kampur. His reply was to the effect that he had already made inquiries as to the possibility of levying an attachment, but he had been compelled to release the little property he had laid hands on, evidence being offered that the real owner was "the Mohammedan prostitute whom he had been passing off as his *brahman* 'wife.'" I did not pass on this last piece of information to the Mission ladies at Rasulabad. Later on I heard from Parmatma Sahai himself, who addressed me a petition through the Superintendent of the jail in which he was confined. He was most anxious to pay his fine: by way of a beginning, if I would be kind enough to address the Superintendent of Police of a certain district, I would find that this gentleman was in possession of a currency note for fifty rupees, the property of the petitioner. I might take this by way of a first instalment. In some bewilderment I addressed the officer concerned. I received in reply a registered packet containing one-half of a currency note for the sum mentioned, with a request for an acknowledgment, and an intimation that the convict might possibly know where the other half was. I never succeeded in entirely clearing up the mystery, or in the efforts I made to induce the Currency Office to pay on the mutilated note; but further correspondence, read in the light of the evidence given by the worthy banker who had appeared before me as a witness for the defence, gave me the bald outline of what must have been quite an interesting story. Some years before, while serving a sentence of imprisonment for another offence, the man whom I knew as Parmatma Sahai had communicated to the local Superintendent of Police an offer to put him on the track of the cleverest gang of forgers in India. As a sample of their work and evidence of his own good faith, he produced one-half of a currency note for fifty rupees, declaring that it was so like a genuine note as to defy detection. He was taken out of the jail to be interviewed by various police officers whom he led a pretty dance for some days. No forgers were ever discovered upon his information, and the mutilated currency note was so astonishingly like a real one because it happened to be a genuine product of the Government press.

This was about the last I heard of Parmatma Sahai. He appealed to the High Court against his conviction and the sentence I had passed on him. The learned Judge who summarily rejected the appeal remarked that the convict's petition was a portentously lengthy document—" much of it grossly scandalous." I have always mildly wondered what it said about me.

V.

TWO FAILURES OF JUSTICE.

LOOKING back on my work as a Sessions Judge, I call to mind a certain number of cases which cost me an expenditure of effort out of all proportion to the results achieved. Few things can be more disheartening than to wrestle with a mass of dubious and largely fabricated evidence, to arrive at the conclusion that a serious crime has undoubtedly been committed, to unravel up to a certain point some ingenious scheme for covering up its traces, only to be driven in the end to a verdict of acquittal, which means that the criminals have had the best of their encounter with the forces of the law. In selecting two curious specimens of this class of case, I find that both of them concern members of the *jat* caste, and that their narration reflects unfavourably on a community for which I entertain the profoundest respect. I ask leave to preface my narrative by making an *amende honorable.*

The *Jats* are an ancient people who seem to have preserved through centuries certain marked racial characteristics. That they should have done so is not surprising, in view of the intensity of their clan feeling and the dourness of their character. I see no reason to doubt the correctness of the theory which identifies them with the Getæ of classical historians. Their name would bulk even larger than it does in the history of India if important sections of their community had not embraced Islam in Sindh and Baluchistan, and Sikhism in the Panjab. As Sikhs they formed the backbone of the stubborn infantry which fought our army to a standstill on the field of Chillianwallah. Those clans which remained within the pale of Hinduism founded dynasties at Bharatpur and Dholpur, and the plundering raids for which they were at one time famous have left them scattered in village settlements beyond the borders of the Panjab and Rajputana, especially in the Meerut and Rohilkhand divisions of the Province of Agra. They are capable of fierce quarrels amongst themselves, especially about land, but the clan will always close its ranks against interference from outside. If one of their faction fights has resulted in the death of one of the combatants, what they really want is to be allowed to settle the matter in their own way, under the direction of their own village elders. The interference of the police may prove to be inevitable, but the evidence laid before the court at the subsequent trial for homicide will often bear less relation to the facts of the case than to what some *panchayat*, or gathering of headmen, has determined to be an appropriate ending to the unfortunate episode.

I can imagine few tasks less enviable than that of a Sub-Inspector of Police entering a *jat* village, resolved to ascertain precisely how and why some sturdy agriculturist of the place came by the fractured skull which has necessitated his investigation. There will be no evidence available but that of caste-fellows of the deceased, and the one thing the unfortunate Police Officer can be certain of is that no one of these will tell him more of the truth than the village council has determined beforehand to disclose.

Now and then the story as laid before the police is doctored to a quite remarkable extent, as the following instance will prove. It was after sunset on a misty evening in August, with the brief Indian twilight rapidly drawing to a close. The residents of the little hamlet of Karela had come in from their fields; lamps were being lighted here and there, as the peasants prepared to settle down for the night. Suddenly they were startled by a violent outcry, apparently proceeding from some point to the west of the village site, where a cart-track wound through a patch of scrub jungle. Shouts of "Help, brothers!" and "Dacoits!" seemed to predominate over the rest of the uproar. Half a dozen villagers snatched up their bamboo staves and hurried in that direction. As they drew nearer they could distinguish the clashing of wooden clubs, fierce exclamations as of men engaged in mortal combat, and a shriller, youthful voice still crying loudly for help. The rescuers burst through the screen of low bushes, to find a large country-cart drawn by two fine oxen standing in the track, and to get a glimpse of the backs of two men rushing round a bend in a direction more or less opposite to that from which they had themselves come. As they started to follow, the two strangers met them, having just turned back. They were profuse in expressions of gratitude. They had been held up by robbers, half a dozen or so, who stopped the cart, told them to get out of it and proposed to search it for any valuables that might be worth carrying off. " The rascals did not know the sort of people they had to deal with. We are *jats* from Phulpur, we do not tamely allow ourselves to be plundered by any riff-raff who think they can do what they like with us if they outnumber us by two to one." The speaker broke off abruptly and hurried towards the cart. " That reminds me," he cried, " they knocked poor uncle down just before they bolted, hearing you people coming up. I greatly fear poor uncle must be hurt." It was even so; in the coarse grass a yard or two from the cart lay a sturdy *jat*, something past the prime of life. His trusty quarterstaff of bamboo had slipped from his hands, and he gave no sign of life. His companions, a powerfully built man of about thirty and a youngster little over half that age, stooped over him in great concern. He was carefully lifted into the cart, which the Karela men guided towards their own hamlet. There it was soon placed beyond doubt that the elderly man was quite dead; he had a nasty wound from some blunt weapon right on the top of the head.

The travellers rested in the village for the night; they needed no entertainment for man or beast. They were on a long journey and carried all supplies with them. Early the next morning they were directed to the nearest police station, where Paltu *jat*, of Phulpur, a village fully twenty miles from Karela, made a formal report. The deceased was his uncle. They had set out together, taking a lad with them to drive the cart, to go to Sultanpur in the Meerut district where they had some business. As a matter of fact Paltu's younger brother had a daughter, whose marriage had with some difficulty been arranged with the son of a landholder of Sultanpur. The bridegroom's family were raising difficulties about sending for the bride. As his uncle had arranged the match in the first instance, it had been decided that he should come along and see what could be done. They had a little bag of money with them in the cart, a present for the bridegroom's people, which it was hoped would smooth out the trouble; that was one reason why they had preferred to put up a fight against long odds, sooner than let the dacoits search the cart. These rascals, there were certainly six of them, if not more, had come upon them all of a sudden as they drove along the village track which they thought would bring them to one of the main roads leading towards the Ganges. Of course, it was very late for them to be travelling over such a lonely path, but this was poor old uncle's fault. He was the only one of the party who had been to Sultanpur before; he professed to know the way, and he must have missed it somewhere. Anyhow, that was what had happened. The dacoits had bolted just as the Karela men came up to the rescue, but one of them had struck uncle down with a terrible blow on the head.

The Sub-Inspector of Police went first to Karela, and he had not been there long before he began to entertain suspicions. The villagers had been talking the matter over amongst themselves, and they were distinctly sceptical on the subject of dacoits. Certainly, they had not seen any; and as their headman shrewdly remarked, what in the name of goodness would dacoits be doing in that forsaken spot? Unless they had been dogging the travellers all the way from Phulpur, they could not conceivably have known that a cart containing booty in its most valuable form—a bag of cash—would be passing that way about nightfall. Moreover, how did the cart come to be there? Travellers who elect to make a long journey by road in August, instead of availing themselves of modern facilities for railway travel, will at least keep as far as possible to the metalled roads. Karela was not even on any plausible short-cut between one main road and another. When Paltu was closely questioned on this point, his answers deepened the mystery. He gave the name of an important village where he said they had halted in the middle of the day; and the Sub-Inspector realised that any cart proceeding from that village to Karela must either have made a quite extraordinary détour, or have crossed an important canal distributary by the only bridge available for a number of miles. A shrewd question disclosed the fact that Paltu did not even know of the existence of the distributary. He could only have avoided it by turning off before he even reached the alleged scene of his mid-day halt, and working round in a certain direction. The Sub-Inspector made a mental note of the fact that this route would bring the travellers to a village, not more than three or four miles from Karela, inhabited by their caste-fellows—the only *jat* village anywhere in that neighbourhood.

It need hardly be said that he made a thorough examination of the scene of the alleged dacoity. The results were not very conclusive. Sherlock Holmes with his magnifying glass might have reconstructed the whole story out of wheel-tracks and footprints in the wayside grass, but no one expects an Indian police officer to rise to such heights. Moreover, there had been a sharp pelt of rain in the early hours of the morning. This was a likely enough occurrence at the season of the year, but it discounted the fact that no blood was to be found at or near the place where the corpse had been lifted from the ground, and that the appearance of the grass there and the bushes around it did not suggest a desperate encounter such as Paltu described. At the *jat* village near Karela the Sub-Inspector drew blank; the whole village with one voice denied having seen anything of their caste-fellows from Phulpur. Nevertheless, inquiries patiently pursued in that neighbourhood resulted in the discovery of fairly convincing evidence that Paltu's cart had been seen at two points along a road which led towards the *jat* village, and had been seen somewhere about sunset at a point between that village and Karela. The Sub-Inspector inclined to the belief that Paltu had, in fact, looked up his caste-fellows, seeking advice or assistance in some scheme that he had in mind. They had presumably declined to do anything for him, beyond, perhaps, suggesting the cart-track that led past Karela as a suitable scene for his intended operation. Nevertheless, they obviously had no intention of giving him away.

It remained to try what could be discovered at Phulpur and at Sultanpur. Here, at anyrate, the Sub-Inspector came upon one thing that he was in search of, traces of a serious dispute within the *jat* community itself. The Sultanpur people were very angry. There had been no marriage, not even a contract of marriage, between any lad of their village and any maiden of Phulpur. It was quite true that a man from that place—they gave the name of the deceased—had once paid them a visit with a view to arranging such a marriage, but they had failed to come to terms. An ancient custom amongst the *Jats* lays it down that the girls of a family must marry into a sept superior to their own; the Sultanpur men occupied that position towards their caste-fellows of Phulpur and could ask something substantial in the way of a 'bridegroom price.' The boy the Phulpur men were making up this story about had since been married elsewhere. It was certainly quite a different story which the Sub-Inspector heard at Phulpur. The people there insisted that a marriage had actually taken place; at anyrate a substantial sum had been fixed as the dowry of Paltu's niece, and an instalment paid over. The Sultanpur family had apparently discovered that they could make better terms elsewhere, and were behaving in the most dishonest fashion.

In fact, the Phulpur men were so indignant that they ended by giving away just a little more than they probably meant to do. Patiently pushing his inquiries in both places, the Sub-Inspector was able to piece together a story which, so far as it went, had a ring of truth about it, and could be substantiated by evidence. The deceased, as one of the leading men of his village and acting on behalf of the whole family, had, in fact, visited Sultanpur in search of a bridegroom for the daughter of his young nephew. He had taken with him a sum of money raised by Paltu and his brother, and this money he at anyrate alleged himself to have paid over to the father of the prospective bridegroom. When the family at Sultanpur broke off the negotiation, having presumably received a better offer from some other quarter, Paltu had demanded the return of his money. There had been quite a sharp altercation in the family, and a *panchayat*, or meeting of the village elders, had undoubtedly been held at Phulpur, on the very day preceding the alleged dacoity at Karela, to settle this dispute. Here, however, the investigation ran up against the blank wall of clan reticence. The Phulpur men insisted that a compromise had been arranged, according to which Paltu and his uncle were to make the journey to Sultanpur together. It was understood that they were to take with them a sum of money and endeavour to persuade the people there to produce another bridegroom, if indeed the lad originally proposed was no longer available. Whether it was Paltu's money or his uncle's that they took with them, nobody professed to know; nor could anyone suggest what had been finally settled regarding Paltu's claim to reimbursement in the event of the further negotiations at Sultanpur leading to no result.

Finally, the much-harrassed Sub-Inspector sent Paltu up for trial on the charge of having murdered his uncle. The lad who had accompanied him to drive the cart was included in the charge, perhaps as a last effort to see whether he could be frightened into offering to give evidence. The police theory was that Paltu had insisted hotly on his claim that his uncle, having allowed those sharpers at Sultanpur to cheat him out of the money, was bound to make it good; that the rejection of this demand had rankled until his anger rose to murderous pitch; that he had proposed the futile journey to Sultanpur as part of a plan for decoying his uncle into a lonely place where he could set upon him, with or without the active assistance of the youngster whom he had roped into the scheme, because his help would in any case be required in order to support the story of a sudden attack by unknown robbers. There was a further suggestion that the bag of money they had with them had, in fact, been provided by the unfortunate uncle, so that Paltu hoped to satisfy his cupidity along with his revenge. According to this theory, the scene of the crime was the bypath near Karela, where Paltu and his young accomplice must have stopped the cart on some pretext or other, induced their unsuspecting relative to dismount, done him to death and made sure that life was extinct, before raising the alarm which brought the residents of the hamlet hastening to the spot.

The only defence actually set up at the trial was the truth of the story of an attack by unknown robbers, as told in the original report to the police. This I was satisfied that the prosecution evidence definitely disproved; the explanations suggested of the various circumstances put forward to demonstrate its falsity were futile and unconvincing. There remained, nevertheless, serious difficulties about the prosecution case. Obviously the story as a whole pre-supposed on the part of the deceased a fatuous trustfulness, in itself hardly believable and in no case to be reconciled with the theory of a violent and deadly quarrel. Then the medical evidence provided a fatal snag. The Civil Surgeon of Moradabad, to whom the corpse had been sent for post mortem examination, was positive that, making every allowance for the rate at which decomposition sets in in that climate and at that season of the year, the man had been dead not less than twenty-four hours before his corpse was carried into the hamlet of Karela.

I took an infinity of trouble over the case. One of the safeguards provided by the Indian Criminal Procedure Code for keeping a check on the proceedings of an investigating police officer requires him to keep a diary of his investigation. I held up the trial until I had studied every word of the Sub-Inspector's diary, and I examined him at length upon certain entries which I found there. I also recalled a number of the prosecution witnesses and questioned them closely with respect to a theory which was steadily gathering shape and consistency in my own mind. I put it beyond doubt that not one of the witnesses by whose evidence the prosecution hoped to trace the progress of the cart between Phulpur and Karela had spoken to the elderly *jat*, or could prove that he was then alive. One or two had noticed only two men in the cart, obviously Paltu and the youth who was driving it; one or two others had noticed a third man in the cart, lying down on the straw and apparently asleep. I put it to the Sub-Inspector whether, in the course of his investigations at Phulpur, he had not found any other *jat* of that village suffering from injuries such as he might have received in a faction fight. Reluctantly that officer admitted (the fact was noted in his diary) that he had seen a young fellow with a broken arm; it was Paltu's own brother, the father of the girl whose marriage was the source of the whole trouble. Here the accused, to the obvious uneasiness of his own counsel, interrupted hotly to say that his brother was present outside the court, that he could swear that his arm had been broken by a kick from a refractory bullock, and other witnesses from the village could prove the fact.

The conclusion I came to was that the homicide under investigation must be put back a whole day, or a day and a half; that the meeting of the elders at Phulpur, so far from bringing about an amicable settlement of the dispute between Paltu and his uncle, had resulted in a faction fight, at the end of which the *jat* community of the place had found itself with a corpse on its hands. The rest of the story was the attempt to dispose of that corpse to the satisfaction of the inquisitive police, who will insist on prying into these matters. It was the corpse which had made the twenty-mile journey, first to the *jat* village near Karela and on to Karela itself. The story of the attack by unknown robbers was the climax of a gallant attempt to retain in the hands of the *jat* community the determination of the suitable penalty to be exacted for the death of a *jat* in the course of a family quarrel.

Indeed, I do not know why I should call it an

'attempt'; in substance it was a complete success. I could not record a conviction of murder on the evidence before me. Counsel for the prosecution made a last appeal to me to hold that Paltu must have killed his uncle, at Phulpur if not at Karela, because even on the theory to which I seemed to incline, it would be the actual murderer on whom the community must lay the burden of the disposal of the corpse. To this I could only reply that one does not hang a man on a slight balance of probability, and after all it may well have been thought that the safest thing was to entrust the job to someone who had not done the killing.

Of course, my friend Paltu remained within the grasp of the law. At the very least he had committed the offence of making a false report at a police station; it might even be possible to secure his conviction for the graver offence of "fabricating false evidence." So far, however, as concerned the death of "poor uncle," he left my court a free man.

The second story which I have to tell is also connected, though in a fashion which may not be immediately apparent, with the difficulties caused in a *jat* household by the presence of a marriageable daughter. Every now and then a Sessions Judge finds on his calendar a case in which the accused is a woman, and the charges against her are (*a*) wilful murder; and (*b*) attempted suicide, the two offences committed in the course of one and the same transaction. He at once knows exactly what to expect. In some family a young wife was desperately unhappy. Possibly her husband was unkind to her; more often she was being bullied and nagged at beyond endurance by her mother-in-law. One morning she rushed out of the house, perhaps honestly bent upon putting an end to her miserable existence, perhaps subconsciously aware that she was only about to register her emphatic protest against injustice in a fashion which her family would not soon forget. In her agitation she disregards the fact that she has a baby in her arms; she makes straight for the nearest well and jumps into it. Quite often, she no sooner finds herself in the water than she screams loudly for help, and clings to the side of the well, if, indeed, the moderate depth of the water does not make this last precaution unnecessary. When people come to pull her out, the baby has somehow been drowned in the water or killed by the shock. Technically she is guilty of the murder of the child, over and above the presumed attempt on her own life.

I feel a certain suspicion that more of these cases occur than ever come into Court for trial. When one of them does, there is usually no defence. The Judge records a conviction on both charges, and on the graver of the two proceeds to pass "the lesser of the two sentences permissible by law"—that of transportation for life. He then sends up a recommendation to mercy to the Local Government, and the sentence is reduced to one of imprisonment for a period which may vary according to the degree of provocation the unfortunate culprit is understood to have received. Yet it was in the trial of one of these apparently simple cases that I found myself seriously perplexed, and, moreover, discovered that my assessors were perfectly certain that they knew all about it.

The accused was a *jat* woman something over twenty years old. The evidence was that she had been seen early one morning coming hastily out of her house, leading by the hand her daughter, a girl between four and five years of age, and carrying in her arms a baby boy of perhaps eighteen months. She went straight to a well at some little distance from her own house, and perhaps thirty or forty yards from a small group of huts inhabited by the village menials. She pushed the girl into the well and jumped in herself, the boy in her arms. Two sweepers, who deposed that they had seen this, rushed towards the spot, raising an alarm. For what followed there was an overwhelming body of evidence. Three or four *jats*, all more or less distant cousins of the woman's husband, had hurried up; and it so happened that they were accompanied by one entirely disinterested witness, a police constable who had arrived in the village that very morning with a summons to serve on one of the residents. The well was a fairly deep one, and the salvage operations took some little time. One of the *jat* witnesses was lowered into the well by a rope. He said he found the woman, in a state of abject terror, clinging to the masonry with one hand and clasping the baby, well above the level of the water, in the other. He rescued the infant first and got him up to the top, none the worse for his adventure. He then tied the rope round the woman's armpits and supported himself without it while she was drawn into safety. He thought at first that his work was done, and was asking for the rope to be let down to him, when someone shouted that the little girl was still in the well. He could see nothing of her; but after one or two attempts succeeded in recovering her dead body from the bottom of the water.

All this was corroborated by a number of witnesses, including the police constable. It was difficult at first sight to see what defence there could be. The accused was represented by counsel, not a very usual circumstance in these cases. He cross-examined the *jat* witnesses as to whether they were not on bad terms with the woman's husband. They admitted that there had been a dispute in the family about the right of succession to certain land. One or two of them said the dispute was no concern of theirs; one or two others confessed that it was, but indignantly denied that any little quarrel of this sort could conceivably have induced them to manufacture the elaborate story with which they had come into court. The two menials were severely cross-examined; they seemed to me obviously uneasy, though this might only be at finding themselves constrained to give evidence which might be considered derogatory to their *jat* masters. They were distinctly hazy about details, and I was inclined to doubt whether one of them had really been looking in the direction of the well at all, until his attention was attracted, perhaps by the sound of the first splash, perhaps by some exclamation on the part of the other. Both of them stoutly insisted, nevertheless, that they had actually seen the accused pushing the little girl into the well. The first real doubt concerning the whole affair stirred in my mind when I came to the medical evidence. The unfortunate child had not been drowned at all; the Civil Surgeon was quite positive that no single one of the characteristic symptoms of death by drowning was discoverable at the post-mortem examination. On the contrary, there was a well-marked wound on the top of the head, and the cause of death was a fractured skull. The injury was one which might have been caused by a blow from a blunt weapon, or by the head striking upon some hard substance in the course of a fall from a considerable height. In the opinion of the medical expert it was impossible to say that the post-mortem symptoms were inconsistent with the theory that the head had come into violent contact with the masonry of the well in the act of falling, but even then it was just a little curious that there was not the slightest indication of an attempt to draw breath after reaching the water.

I turned to the accused; she met the entire story with a series of sullen denials. She had never been in the well at all, nor had the little boy. She had not the faintest idea how her daughter had been killed. She had last seen the child playing about in front of the house. There had been a hullabaloo a little later, and the corpse had been brought to her door by some people who were saying that they had found it in the well. For aught she knew the little girl might have fallen in; the well was a dangerous one, the mouth insufficiently raised above the surface of the ground. She remembered having warned the child not to go too near it. As for the rest of the story it was an invention of the *jat* cousins, out of spite against her husband; they had just done it to worry him. It was not even true that she was unhappy at home; of course, her mother-in-law had a temper and had spoken sharply to her once or twice, but nothing to make a fuss about. Asked what she had to say about the police constable's evidence, she answered sulkily that you can always bribe a constable.

I got the woman's husband into the witness-box; he seemed distinctly worried about the whole business, but had little enough to say that was of any use. He himself had been about his work in a field a long way from the village site; by the time he came on the scene they had got his daughter's body out. His wife was sitting somewhere near, nursing the little boy to stop him from crying. So far as he could remember her clothes were wet, but really he had been too much upset to notice details. He had no great opinion of the 'cousins' who had given evidence in the case; two of them had certainly tried to do him down over a dispute in which the right was entirely on his side. Still, he would not go the length of accusing them of having invented this whole story; besides, if the constable said he saw the woman being drawn up out of the well, he supposed it must have been so. As for domestic unhappiness, he knew little or nothing. His mother and his wife did wrangle from time to time as women will do; a wise man took no more notice of such matters than he could help.

When the case came to be argued, the counsel for the accused put up a fairly good fight, but it was on the lines of his client's own statement. The little girl must have fallen into the dangerous well while playing about near it. The feud in the village had suggested to the malevolent cousins the idea of taking advantage of the accident to make trouble for the family. Perhaps he might be permitted to go a little beyond the story told by his own client. It was conceivable that she had seen the accident, had jumped into the well to rescue her daughter, and was now afraid to admit this fact, seeing the use her husband's enemies were making of it. He did not desire to suggest that the police constable was deliberately bolstering up a false case, but the court must allow for the tendency men of this class have to magnify their office, to assign to themselves the leading part in any affair in which they have been concerned. The probability was that the man had come upon the scene a little later than he said he did, and could not resist the temptation to describe as events which had actually taken place under his very eyes things which he had been told by the bystanders on his arrival.

In summing up the case to the Assessors I pointed out that the prosecution and the defence were at one in making light of the difficulty presented by the medical evidence; they both asked the court, in effect, to believe that the child's death was caused by her head striking against the masonry of the well as she fell into it. If this were accepted as true, it was difficult to discredit the solid body of evidence on which the prosecution rested. When, however, I asked for their opinion as to whether the charges of murder and attempted suicide were proved against the accused, both Assessors replied in the negative, with a certain emphasis which showed that they had not a shadow of a doubt in their own minds.

"Very well," said I, "can you give me your reasons for this opinion?" The elder Assessor looked at me with an air of mild surprise.

"Your Honour," he said, "it was a little girl."

"Quite so," I replied, and waited for more.

"Also, these people are *jats*," added the old gentleman. His companion broke in with a touch of eagerness. "And the Doctor Sahib saw quite clearly that the girl was not drowned at all. Of course, the little boy was not hurt in the least."

"No doubt," added the first Assessor, "everything would have been very different if the constable had not arrived in the village that morning."

There was no mistaking what these worthy gentlemen had in their minds: take the story as they saw it. You have a *jat* family with a daughter rapidly approaching marriageable age. By what has been called the custom of 'hypergamy,' the respectability of the family is involved in finding a bridegroom for her in a sept higher than their own. It may be that feelers have been thrown out, negotiations attempted, sufficient to prove that this is going to be a ruinously expensive business. The birth of a baby brother has made the father desperately reluctant to encumber the little family estate with a hopeless load of debt. There is no need to imagine a premeditated and cold-blooded murder. We may rather postulate prolonged discussions, a family conclave in which brothers and cousins are appealed to for assistance which they decline to give. The thing has become a rankling sore in the family life, a subject continually cropping up and never to be mentioned without loss of temper. At last someone is exacerbated beyond endurance. Or it may be that some trifling provocation given by the wretched girl herself provokes a blow in which is concentrated the smouldering rancour of months. One way or another a savage blow is struck, and it is known in the village that there has been a sudden death in the house of such-an-one. Ordinarily the village watchman would have reported, on his next monthly visit to the police station, a death from malarial fever or possibly from snake-bite, and that would have been the end of the matter. By a perverse stroke of ill-fortune, before the poor little corpse has even been disposed of, a constable comes blundering in on a piece of routine duty. Beyond this it becomes largely a matter of speculation how far the unwelcome visitor could be hoodwinked, or what price he would ask for connivance, or even active assistance, while an elaborate comedy is staged. In any case, a paternal government has a way of dealing very gently with women who kill their children in an attempt to take their own lives. The mother can be bullied into acquiescence, even supposing—and it is a possible theory—that it was not she herself who, goaded to madness by taunts and recriminations, had struck the fatal blow. The corpse can be flung into the well; the mother must be lowered down gently, especially if she is to take the baby boy with her, and just give him one souse in the water, "to add verisimilitude to an otherwise bald and unconvincing narrative." Then you can raise as much outcry as you please; let the constable come bustling up and supervise the salvage operations. Later on, you must find a lawyer to defend the woman; someone knows of a smart fellow at Moradabad, perhaps capable even of persuading the Judge Sahib to let the accused off altogether, even though her defence may be about as far from the truth as the evidence for the prosecution.

Well—I do not say positively that this is what had happened, but what was I to do with the evidence before me, and the almost contemptuously positive opinion of the two Assessors? I recorded a verdict of acquittal, and recommended a fresh investigation. Nothing ever came of this. The whole village stood by the story as told at the trial. The police remained of the opinion that a perfectly straightforward case had been spoilt, because there happened to be a queer accident about the actual manner of death, and because the Judge Sahib had allowed himself to be influenced by a crazy notion which had somehow got into the heads of a couple of stupid Assessors. I can only say that they struck me as shrewd and intelligent gentlemen; they were both of them landholders in a small way, one a *brahman* the other a Mohammedan, and presumably capable of forming a sound conclusion as to what might conceivably happen in a village community under given circumstances.

Having said this much, I feel bound to add a word or two on the subject of female infanticide. When I commenced my Indian service, over forty years ago now, there were districts in my part of India where some few castes retained an unenviable reputation in this matter. Even then, those who had devoted much attention to the subject believed that anything like the deliberate putting out of existence of unwanted girls was extremely rare. What did remain was a tendency in the direction of callous neglect. Year by year the recorded mortality from fever, or diseases connected with malnutrition, was suspiciously high amongst girls below a certain limit of age, in particular parts of the province and amongst particular castes. The matter was dealt with by drawing up a list of 'infanticide villages,' and quartering punitive police upon them until such time as the residents could be proved to have mended their ways. The salaries of these policemen were recovered by a small rate levied upon the black-listed villages, and collected along with the Land Revenue. I write without having access to the latest statistics, but my own belief is that this simple measure has proved thoroughly effective. The villagers hated having to pay the extra tax, and simply loathed the continual presence in their midst of strange constables. Whenever it fell to my duty to make a tour of 'infanticide villages,' and check by actual enumeration the proportion of males to females amongst infants below a certain age, I was welcomed with enthusiasm in any village where the inhabitants knew that they had at last managed to bring up the number of girls to the required proportion, and that my report would result in the removal of the detested incubus. Proud fathers hastened into the sacred interior of their homes to produce their offspring for inspection. May I add, without bringing a blush to the cheek of modesty, that my instructions were to leave no room for imposture in connection with the said inspection? The villagers had their own little jokes on the subject, frankly Rabelaisian, but taken in the best possible part by everyone concerned.

VI.

CHAURI CHAURA.

CHAPTER I.

THE STORY OF THE RIOT.

THE railway station of Chauri Chaura lies some fifteen miles south of Gorakhpur, the headquarters of the district of that name, in the north of the Province of Agra. It has been named, in the alliterative Indian fashion, after twin villages, of which Chaura is the more important and contains the police station, the scene of the tragedy I am undertaking to describe. The events which took place there on the afternoon of the 4th February, 1922, cannot be made intelligible without some allusion to the general condition of Indian politics at the time. For two years previously the Government of India had been confronted by two distinct agitations, working in somewhat precarious alliance.

The first of these was a movement of non-co-operation, or passive resistance, the leader of which was a gentleman, formerly a Barrister of one of our Inns of Court, now an ascetic and devotee, known to his fellow-countrymen as 'Mahatma' Gandhi. To judge him by his published utterances, he is an idealist whose mind is fixed upon a picture it has formed of the India of a long-past Golden Age. It centres round the self-contained village community, growing its own food irrespective of the demands of any export trade, and supplying all its simple wants by the home manufactures of its own artisans. The existing Government of India is to him, not merely an alien rule, but intrinsically 'Satanic,' the very antithesis and negation of his ideal of rustic happiness. He sees clearly enough that it could not continue to exist for a day without the co-operation of Indians themselves. At an early stage of his movement he called upon all Indian officials to resign their posts, title-holders to resign their titles and decorations, lawyers to cease from practising in courts of law, students to desert their colleges and universities. Behind all this lies the threat to organise 'civil disobedience,' a vast movement of passive resistance to all enforcement of the existing law, including the non-payment of taxes and of the agricultural rents from which Government derives the bulk of its income in the form of Land Revenue. The great revolution, however, is to be accomplished wholly by 'soul force,' by absolute non-violence, by a people trained and disciplined to submit passively to all punishment, to all forms of coercion, by which the established Government may seek to vindicate its authority.

The leader of this movement laboured hard to establish a working alliance between his followers and the wholly different organisation which was seeking to voice the grievances of his Mohammedan fellow-countrymen. This was commonly spoken of as the 'Khilāfat' movement. The name is the Indian form of the word 'Caliphate,' and it implies that those who adopted it were concerned with the treatment meted out to the Sultan of Turkey, as Caliph of Islam, in the settlement which followed on the World War. I am here touching on the verge of a subject which would require a long chapter to itself, if I were to attempt to handle it at all adequately. I must be content to say that few Englishmen seem to me to have any conception of the strain thrown on the loyalty of Indian Moslems by the treatment meted out to Turkey after the War. The mere delay in settling any terms of peace at all was in itself a disastrous blunder; the attempt to leave the Sultan in possession of Constantinople, but hedged in by conditions and restrictions derogatory to his status as an independent Sovereign, was worse; but the intrusion of the Greeks into Asia Minor was worst of all—an incredible piece of stupidity for which we have paid our price in more ways than one. As if all this were not enough, the settlement effected in Arabia ignored the fact that the custody of the Holy Places of Islam was a matter of vital concern to Mohammedans all the world over. Since the days of which I am writing, Ghazi Kemal and Ibn Sàud have between them so altered the whole situation that it is idle to pursue the subject further. I can only stress the fact that during the years 1920 and 1921, serious discontent towards the British Government was widely, and not unreasonably, prevalent amongst Indian Moslems generally.

This much premised, I may return to Gorakhpur and invite the reader's attention to matters which came to my knowledge in the course of a strenuous month's work, during which I sat with my honoured chief, Sir Grimwood Mears, to dispose of the appeals of one hundred and seventy peasants of that district, then lying under sentence of death.

In the month of February, 1921, Mahatma Gandhi had paid a personal visit to the Gorakhpur district. It is clear that he left behind him a profound impression. To the Hindu peasants he was an incarnation of their ideal of the ascetic and saint; they ascribed to him in all sincerity superhuman powers. He carried with him the promise of the speedy inauguration of a new era, a Golden Age of rural felicity. He succeeded also in giving effect to his plans for a working alliance between his own followers and the discontented Moslems, at least to this extent, that he left behind him a single organisation known as the 'National Volunteers,' in place of the separate associations which were working elsewhere under the divergent titles of 'Congress Volunteers' and 'Khilāfat Volunteers.'

Apparently this was the weapon by the gradual

perfecting of which the great revolution was to be accomplished. For the existing Government there was to be substituted a system vaguely apprehended under the name of *Swarāj*, literally 'self-rule.' To the educated Indian the word was capable of covering many shades of meaning from 'self-government' to 'independence.' It was interesting to examine the mass of evidence produced at the subsequent trial in the endeavour to ascertain what the word conveyed to the peasantry of Gorakhpur. Mere discontent with the existing order was expressed by the witness who told the Court frankly that he understood it to mean "the rule of someone else." To the majority, however, the word was indissolubly connected with the impression left on their minds by the commanding personality of Mr Gandhi himself: it was 'Gandhiji's Swarāj,' or the 'Mahatmaji's Swarāj,' for which they looked. It was to be a millennium, in which taxation would be limited to the collection of small cash contributions, or dues in kind, from fields and threshing-floors, and the tillers of the soil would hold their lands at little more than nominal rentals. Naturally enough, there was to be some special reward for those prepared to come forward at once and work for the attainment of the ideal; when the day of triumph came, those who had been enrolled as Volunteers would each receive the comfortable living wage of twelve rupees a month. As a step in the right direction, the organisation was to set itself, in every way possible, to supplant by co-operative effort the existing machinery of Government. The Volunteers were taught to police their own villages, and tribunals were set up to which the peasants were urged to refer their disputes, in place of the existing courts of justice. Considerable efforts were made to give the movement a semi-military organisation, both by placing the Volunteers under a regular hierarchy of local and superior command, and by teaching them the elements of drill. It is fair to note that this drilling did not include any form of exercise in the use of weapons; it was confined to practice in marching in regular formation, starting, halting, and turning back in response to signals given by the sound of whistles.

The absence of weapons was an integral part of the system as conceived by its founder. Every Volunteer on enrolment set his thumb impression to a 'pledge form,' in which the duty of absolute non-violence under all circumstances was laid down in stringent terms. Along with this, however, there was an unqualified undertaking that the individual Volunteer should obey without question the orders of his 'officers,' and the prohibition against violence was qualified by the condition that it was to endure only so long as non-violence continued to be the policy of the 'nation.' Obviously, a given body of Volunteers would only require to be told by its 'officers' that the time for action had now come, and these would find themselves at the head of an organised body of men, pledged to obey their orders and capable of military manœuvring of an elementary kind. The *lathi*, or quarterstaff of bamboo, is the national weapon of the peasant of Northern India; it is to be found in every household and its owner needs no training in its effective use.

These Volunteer organisations had been quietly throwing out their tentacles over the villages of the Gorakhpur district for at least nine months, before any action of a repressive character was undertaken by the constituted authorities. It was at the end of November, 1921, that a notification appeared in the Provincial 'Gazette,' by which the Governor in Council declared "the associations at present known by the names of Khilāfat Volunteers, Congress Volunteers, and National Volunteers," to be "unlawful associations," under a Statute of 1908 which gave the Government certain special powers for the preservation of public order. That the proclamation was technically within the powers of the local Government was never denied. What Nationalist politicians contended was that the special powers conferred by the Act of 1908 were never intended to be exercised against an association the members of which stood pledged to absolute non-violence. The enrolment of National Volunteers continued, and a special form was introduced which purported to bind any person enrolled thereunder to a full knowledge and understanding of the 'Gazette' notification and its legal consequences.

I believe I am doing no more than justice to the leaders who thus challenged the authority of the established Government, when I say that they probably expected the next move to be the wholesale arrest and prosecution of enrolled Volunteers. It is a matter of inference on my part that the consequences anticipated to follow upon this were, first, a deepening of the general discontent on which the agitators relied for ultimate success, and secondly, a striking demonstration of the efficiency of 'soul force,' in the sight of hundreds of peasants cheerfully submitting to a qualified martyrdom for the good of the cause.

The Government, however, held its hand. From the point of view of the organisers of the 'Volunteer' movement it must have been obvious that the instrument they were elaborately fashioning must be put to some immediate and effective use, if it were not to rust and disintegrate in mere idleness. A campaign against licensed shops for the sale of liquor and intoxicating drugs could not fail to suggest itself as a convenient object for the activities of Volunteer associations. It was bound to challenge the attention of the local authorities, yet it could be presented in a form calculated to attract public sympathy and could be undertaken, ostensibly at anyrate, without departure from the principle of non-violence. The actual course of events, however, suggests a doubt whether it was not found that this object, admirable in itself, failed to arouse an adequate measure of spontaneous enthusiasm amongst the Volunteers themselves. At anyrate it was in effect coupled with another, better calculated to appeal to their personal sympathies. The peasantry were suffering from the high prices of provisions, and in the mood to believe that vendors of foodstuffs were trading on their necessities in a fashion which we have come to describe by the word 'profiteering.' Any movement against the prices of food grains would conflict with the interests of peasants who were producers as well as consumers, but it was easy to concentrate the general discontent against the vendors of meat and of fish. It became a watchword amongst the local Volunteers that these should be called upon to reduce their prices 80 or 90 per cent., under the threat that otherwise steps would be taken to prevent them from selling anything at all.

The next point was to select a definite place for the inauguration of the campaign. In this matter it is probable that local rivalries and animosities had some influence in directing the choice. A force having been called into existence which was outside the limits of the law, it was natural that individuals should endeavour to divert its energies into channels innocuous to themselves and perhaps harmful to personal rivals. In one way or another, attention was concentrated on the village of Mundera, a little to the north of Chaura police station, where a market was held twice a week, on Wednesdays and Saturdays. About the end of January, 1922, word went out that the local Volunteers were to 'stop the sale' of country spirits, toddy, hemp drugs, meat and fish in the Mundera bazaar.

The next step on the downward path was the discovery by the Volunteers that they could effect nothing substantial unless they were prepared to act in overwhelming numbers. I quote the following, with slight verbal alterations, from the appellate judgment of the Allahabad High Court.

"On the occasion of the Wednesday market—the 1st February 1922,—a body of Volunteers, thirty to forty in number, moved upon Mundera and halted outside the village, waiting to commence operations as soon as the bazaar was fairly under way. The shopkeepers and the agents of the local landholders were on the alert. The latter came out and questioned the Volunteers, telling them bluntly that Babu Sant Bakhah Singh would allow no interference with his market. Reading a little between the lines of the evidence we infer that any attempt at actual coercion on the part of the Volunteers would have been resisted by force. Word must also have been sent to the police station, for Sub-Inspector Gupteshar Singh marched into Mundera with a considerable body of police constables and village watchmen. Before his arrival, however, the Volunteers had abandoned their enterprise. In face of the resolute attitude of the agents in charge of the bazaar they felt themselves to be too few in number to attempt anything. They scattered, and most of them returned to their homes. Before they went off, however, their leaders distinctly asserted that they proposed to return on the following market day (Saturday, 4th February) in such numbers as to enforce compliance with their demands. There is naturally some room for controversy as to the precise language used; but that a threat was conveyed and was understood as such, is proved by direct evidence and by the fact that the landholder sent a trusted agent to Gorakhpur to appeal to the District Magistrate for special protection for his market on the following Saturday. This resulted in the arrival by train at Chauri Chaura railway station, at about 9 A.M. on the 4th of February, of a small body of armed police, nine muskets in all."

Amongst the leaders of the small company of Volunteers who had thus assembled on the Wednesday morning was one, Bhagwan, an individual who now becomes of importance in the story. He was of the *ahir*, or herdsman caste, had seen service during the war as a member of a labour corps in Mesopotamia, and was consequently in the enjoyment of a small pension. On the strength of his military experience he had been appointed drill instructor to the Volunteers in the neighbourhood of Chaura. This man, along with perhaps three or four of his companions, entered Mundera after the rest had dispersed.

The judgment of the High Court continues :—

" There is no evidence worth speaking of that these men actually did anything provocative, but their mere presence in the bazaar produced unfortunate consequences. Sub-Inspector Gupteshar Singh had reached Mundera under the impression of an emergency calling for action on his part, and he found the persons in charge of the bazaar excited and alarmed. There is some conflict of evidence as to the details of what followed. Indeed, the one witness from whom one would have expected a clear and coherent account, Police Constable Siddiq, the one constable who survived the massacre, is confused and self-contradictory. Taking the evidence as a whole, it seems clear that the Sub-Inspector was, at some time in the forenoon, at the office of the local landholder when certain Volunteers were brought before him by constables who had found them in the bazaar. There were probably only two of them, there may have been three or four, but one of them was certainly Bhagwan *ahir* the 'drill-instructor.' The Sub-Inspector spoke roughly to them, his wrath being directed particularly against Bhagwan, whom he abused for drawing a pension from Government while taking an active part in an unlawful association. There is an allegation that Bhagwan answered insolently; there is also a suggestion that Gupteshar Singh was further inflamed against the man by one of the landholder's agents. What we are certain of is that the Sub-Inspector thoroughly lost his temper and struck Bhagwan; we hold it proved that he gave him two cuts with a light cane, and he very probably also struck him with the open hand. Bhagwan and any Volunteer with him thereupon left Mundera altogether. No arrests were considered necessary by the Sub-Inspector and no official report was ever made as to any collision on that date between the police and the Volunteers. A curious fact is that we have it, not only from the evidence of Siddiq, but from a statement made by Bhagwan himself, that the latter voluntarily presented himself at the police station the following morning (2nd February) and had an explanation with Sub-Inspector Gupteshar Singh. As might be expected, the accounts of this explanation differ somewhat, but they agree to this extent, that apologies were tendered and received and that, as between the principal actors, the unfortunate episode seemed to have been brought to a conclusion satisfactory to both parties."

There were, however, other persons to whose minds the incident presented itself as a lever which might, perhaps, be worked with impressive results. I must warn the reader that for what took place between the afternoon of 1st February and the morning of 4th February we have to rely, in part on the statement of an approver who had turned King's evidence in the hope of saving his own neck, and in part on the reluctant testimony of witnesses whom the High Court judgment describes as being "as economical of the truth as they dared." There is reason to believe that the approver, a man named Shikari, was telling the truth when he described two informal meetings of leaders of the local Volunteers, which took place at his house on the Wednesday evening and on the Thursday morning, 1st and 2nd February. It was determined that letters should be sent out to Volunteer associations in neighbouring villages, with a view to their assembling in a body strong enough to warrant them in paying a visit to the Sub-Inspector at Chaura Police Station, and "asking him why he had beaten our men." It was agreed that a place must be fixed for the rendezvous, not too near Chaura, lest the Sub-Inspector should break up the gathering by arresting the Volunteers piecemeal as they arrived, but within convenient marching distance. The choice fell upon a threshing-floor at a village of the name of Dumri, about a couple of miles from Chaura. The organisers had not forgotten their differences with the shopkeepers of Mundera. The meeting was accordingly fixed for the morning of Saturday, 4th February, and the plan was formulated that the Volunteers should first settle their quarrel with Sub-Inspector Gupteshar Singh, and then proceed northwards to Mundera and impose their will on the licensed vendors and the sellers of meat and fish in the bazaar there. The leaders being illiterate peasants, the services of a schoolboy of eleven were enlisted to write out the necessary letters. To the best of his recollection, the following is a summary of what he wrote :—

> "The Sub-Inspector of Chaura seeks out and beats the Volunteers; therefore bring all your Volunteers to Dumri. We will go and inquire from the Sub-Inspector why he makes a practice of beating the Volunteers; if he wants to send us to jail or to arrest us he may do so with all of us."

All that need be said at present in the way of comment is that it was never proved that the Sub-Inspector had assaulted any Volunteers except Bhagwan, also that the arrest or imprisonment of a compact and unanimous body of anything from one to two thousand men was an obvious impossibility. In this lies the importance of the suggestion that the Volunteers should insist that whatever was done to any one of them should be done to all. The obvious way of dealing with a mob of demonstrators acting outside the limits of the law is to arrest the ringleaders and disperse the rest; there must be no submitting to anything of this sort.

Another step was taken at the same time, regarding which the most searching investigation failed to elicit the whole truth. It has been pointed out that the 'National Volunteers' represented a coalition between the followers of Mahatma Gandhi and the discontented Moslems. There were at Gorakhpur two distinct bodies, either of which might claim a right of control over their movements. One was the Committee of the National Congress and the other the Khilāfat Committee. It was to the latter that the Volunteers with whom we are concerned appealed for guidance. Two of the most active of the local leaders, Nazar Ali and Lal Mohammed, were Moslems who would naturally turn to the representatives of their own faith. Apart from this, I have always wondered how far the fact that the contemplated action was directed against a Hindu Sub-Inspector influenced the course of events. After the consummation of the tragedy which was now maturing, there appeared in an Indian newspaper an appreciative and affecting obituary notice of Sub-Inspector Gupteshar Singh. He was a young man of good family and owed his position to the fact that he had received an education superior to the generality of his class. He was certainly regarded as an able and promising officer. There was some conflict of evidence later on as to whether Lal Mohammed went in person to Gorakhpur. The High Court judgment sums up the facts established by reliable evidence in the following words :—

"Lal Mohammed did cause to be conveyed to the office of the Khilāfat Committee a letter or report, of which one of the exhibits before us is either the original or a correct transcript. This report was sent in by hand so that the information it conveyed could be, and undoubtedly was, supplemented by oral communication with the person or persons who carried it. The report called for an immediate answer: if any written answer was returned it has disappeared, nor can any trace of it be discovered in the correspondence registers of the Gorakhpur Kilāfat Committee. Some sort of answer, oral or written or both, was unquestionably returned."

The 'exhibit' above referred to was to the effect that two Volunteers, while peacefully engaged about their own marketing (the name of the bazaar is not given), had been seized and severely beaten by the officer in charge of the local police station. "We therefore report this matter to your Worships," the letter continues, "in order that you may come and investigate the matter. It is because of your Worships that we Volunteers have not committed any offence of any sort, for whatever action we take will be after inquiring from you, our superiors." The evidence given by members of the Khilāfat Committee at the subsequent trial was that a reply was returned, to the effect that the Volunteers should be patient; if so, the advice was of small effect.

From early morning on Saturday, 4th February, the threshing-floor at Dumri was a busy scene. The local Volunteers arranged the ground, sacking being spread to provide sitting accommodation for the central group of leaders. Some modest provision was made for refreshments in the way of baskets full of raw sugar. Flowers were collected and made into garlands for the adornment of those whom the assembly might desire to honour. In distant villages the Volunteers who had been summoned by letter were mustering in little groups of half a dozen or so, and marching for the appointed rendezvous. From about seven in the morning the converging streams began to flow into Dumri. Harpal, the village watchman, waited until two or three hundred men had gathered, ascertained from the general trend of the conversation that a march on Mundera bazaar was contemplated, and slipped away to Chaura police station with the news. Before the proceedings closed the assembly exceeded a thousand men.

Those responsible for the assembly were bound to wait until they had collected an adequate force ; it was also necessary that a plan of operations should be determined upon and should receive general assent. Most important of all it was to rouse the spirit of the crowd, until its leaders could rely on their unflinching resolution. There were curious indications in the evidence subsequently produced that the local organisers were expecting instructions from headquarters. A certain *brahman*, of the name of Jagat Narayan, had hurried to the spot because, according to his own account, he had formed a low opinion of the character of the local Volunteers, and was persuaded that they were going to get themselves into trouble by acting contrary to the true precepts of non-violence as laid down by 'Mahatmaji' Gandhi. He was cordially received on his first arrival, was garlanded and permitted to address the meeting. When, however, he tried to persuade the gathering to break up, appealing to the principles of 'Gandhiji,' and warning his hearers of the arrival at Chaura of a body of armed police, he met with violent opposition, especially from Nazar Ali and Lal Mohammed. He was told that he was no better than a police spy, his voice drowned in derisive handclapping, and himself finally turned out of the meeting with contumely. Another gentleman, who had been drawn to the spot by the fact that he was interested in certain contracts connected with the Mundera Bazaar, and who was apparently mistaken at first for an emissary from Gorakhpur, spoke to the same effect, and with like unsuccess. Nazar Ali, who seems to have more and more taken the lead, eventually carried the entire meeting with him in a resolution that they were to march, first to Chaura, to settle their quarrel with the Sub-Inspector; and thence to the bazaar at Mundera to stop the sale of intoxicants, of meat, and of fish. No one was to start on the expedition who was not prepared to venture his life on the hazard. A form of oath was administered: anyone who, after setting forth with the rest, turned back before the bullets of the police was to be considered, if a Hindu, to have eaten cow's flesh; if a Mohammedan, the flesh of swine. An even coarser form of the imprecation ran from mouth to mouth amongst the outcasts who formed a large proportion of the crowd, men whose social status could scarcely be degraded by the eating of any kind of flesh.

It would seem, however, that these illiterate peasants were not left wholly without guidance or stimulus from minds better instructed than their own. An episode was spoken of which strikes me as so significant that I prefer to record it as it was narrated by men who were undoubtedly present at Dumri. The drill-instructor, Bhagwan, made a statement to a Magistrate, in the course of which he said :—

" Two Mohammedans wearing spectacles came there. They began to sing songs describing the deeds of Shaukat Ali and Mohammed Ali " (the leaders of the Khilāfat movement). " On hearing the song all became angry, and said, ' Come, we will all go to the police station.' "

In a statement similarly made by another accused occur the words :—

" Two Mohammedans came there. One of them was wearing spectacles and the other had a beard. They came there and began to sing. After this all the Volunteers, who were about three thousand, got up and started from that place crying, ' Victory to Mahatma Gandhi.' "

Another accused, of the name of Raghubir, was a *sunār* or goldsmith, by caste a man of higher social position than most of his fellows. This was his account of the episode :—

" Lectures were delivered. There was a Babu who in his lecture said that we should not go either to Mundera Bazaar or to the police station; if we went in a body there would be a riot. But no one listened to him. A Mohammedan gentleman, whose name and residence I do not know, delivered a lecture, and asked his hearers if they were ready to die. They replied that they were ready. Then all started from there."

The approver, Shikari, deposed as follows before the Sessions Judge:—

"Two other men came, one wearing green glasses, who was of my stature but older, about thirty-two, who from his words appeared to be a Mohammedan. The other was younger than I; I cannot say whether he was a Hindu or a Musalman. The man with glasses began to read from a slip of paper, singing, 'We are going for two years each.' We understood by this 'going to jail.' Then Nazar Ali stood up and publicly administered an oath."

Some months earlier, in a statement which he made before a Magistrate, while his recollection of the events was fresher, Shikari described this episode somewhat differently.

"In the meantime," he said, "two Mohammedans, one of whom was wearing spectacles, came there. I do not know their place of residence. They took out a piece of paper and began to read from it. Then they began to sing. In this song the names of Mohammed Ali and Shaukat Ali were uttered again and again, and it was about their imprisonment. After singing the song they went away to the west. Then we got up and, passing along the raised borders of the fields, reached the road."

Some readers may find it difficult to believe that all the resources of the Criminal Investigation Department, directed by an officer of proved ability in the unravelling of political conspiracies, failed to establish the identity of the two strangers whose voices thus stirred the emotions and clinched the resolution of the crowd; but the result is characteristic of much in our Indian administration. "If ever," said one of the most famous of our Lieutenant-Governors to me, "we come to utter grief in India, it will be from want of knowing what is going on."

I must now ask the attention of the reader to a little geography. The road referred to in Shikari's statement, on which the Volunteers were mustered in some sort of rough formation, is a broad highway running from Gorakhpur to Deoria; though unmetalled, it is one of the principal thoroughfares of the district. Chaura Police Station lay rather less than two miles to the east of the point where the Volunteers formed up. At a point roughly about half-way between the two places lies the small bazaar of Bhopa; here a road branches off to the left, that is to say in a northerly direction, leading to a railway crossing, and beyond that to the bazaar of Mundera. This is the route which the crowd must have followed if their purpose had been limited to carrying out the threat with which some of their leaders had parted from the shopkeepers of Mundera on the previous Wednesday. By ignoring this route and pressing on directly to the east, the crowd showed unmistakably that their first business was with the police station. This lies in an angle where a short length of metalled road turns northward from the Gorakhpur-Deoria highway, and leads to another railway crossing beyond which lies the bazaar of Chaura and a road leading to Mundera. The police station enclosure extends practically from the highway to the railway line; its entrance is on the east side, on to the strip of metalled road, across which lie a few buildings, including the private quarters of the Sub-Inspector.

On the main highway Bhagwan had exerted himself to get the demonstrators into some sort of formation. Flags which had been prepared beforehand were sent to the front, and the crowd marched under the control of officers who from time to time halted them and moved them on again by the sound of whistles. They were in a mood of high excitement, continually raising triumphant cries and acclamations. All along the route their numbers were increasing, in part, no doubt, because small contingents of Volunteers who had been late for the rendezvous at Dumri were joining the line of march, but principally, it is to be feared, by reason of disorderly elements ready enough to contribute their weight to a movement obviously directed against the police, and promising disorder and possible opportunities for plunder. According to the best estimates that could be formed from the evidence, the crowd which started from Dumri was close upon fifteen hundred men; at Bhupa Bazaar there were fully two thousand five hundred; and when the crowd came to a temporary halt at a certain factory, about within sight of the police station, their numbers had risen to over three thousand.

Sub-Inspector Gupteshar Singh was in an unenviable position. He had information as to the movements of the crowd. The village watchman of Dumri had given him early warning that a demonstration in force against the shopkeepers of Mundera was being organised. A friendly landholder, after witnessing the first part of the proceedings at the Dumri gathering, had hastened to Chaura, deeply impressed with the numbers and the resolute spirit of the Volunteers. He earnestly advised the Sub-Inspector to bow his head to the storm and 'let the day go by.' A servant of the landholder of Mundera, who had interviewed the leaders of the demonstration at Bhopa, came hastening in with later news. He came away with the impression that there were already something like four thousand men, marching along like an army, the leaders carrying flags and the crowd raising shouts of "Victory!" Nazar Ali had received his remonstrances with insolence, adding, with obvious irony and a glance at the excited throng at his back, that he was coming on to the police station to ask for a beating. What was the Sub-Inspector to do? More than a year later, after patiently reviewing the entire evidence, two Judges of the High Court formulated the conclusion that the crowd of demonstrators, from the moment they left Dumri, constituted an 'unlawful assembly,' whom it was not merely the right, but the obvious duty, of the police to disperse, using for that purpose whatever degree of force might be indispensably necessary. Could Gupteshar Singh be certain beforehand that this would be the view of the highest judicial tribunal? In any case, what precise degree of force was he to employ? If he opened fire on the mob was he prepared to face the outcry that would follow, the wild stories of the massacre by police muskets of a crowd of peaceful and unarmed demonstrators? For those who had organised the demonstration knew what they were about: the influence of Mahatma Gandhi had prevailed to this extent, that the Volunteers had been mustered at the rendezvous without weapons of any sort, unless the flags carried by the leaders were mounted on poles capable of being used as such in case of need. This remark, of course, does not apply to the miscellaneous riff-raff who had been steadily adding themselves to the flanks and rear of the procession; but it must be frankly written down as a triumph for the Gandhi spirit that it had brought the handful of police face to face with a demonstration, overwhelming in numbers, dangerous to a degree because of the spirit of fierce determination to which the mass had been wrought up, and the disorderly elements which had adhered to it, yet fairly describable as 'a crowd of unarmed peasants.'

The situation made its demands on the physical, as well as the moral, courage of the Sub-Inspector. He had drawn up his men in a position which was strategically sound; his little force stood across the broad highway, denying the crowd, unless it could be brushed aside, access to the police station itself, to the road leading northward in the direction of Mundera, and to the railway line. The extreme importance of this last consideration was soon to be proved by the event. For practical purposes Gupteshar Singh's force consisted of nine muskets of the armed police. These were ancient rifles, roughly adapted for use with either ball cartridge or buck-shot, the cartridges indifferently loaded with reduced charges of powder. Later on, the Judges of the High Court expressed themselves as "satisfied that these were singularly inefficient weapons to be placed in the hands of men expected to deal with a really determined attack delivered by vastly superior numbers." The four or five men of the civil police whom the Sub-Inspector had kept about him were no real addition to his fighting force. Over and above these, he had with him some forty village watchmen, armed with their brass-bound staves of bamboo, but wholly untrained for acting together in a body. If the Sub-Inspector had continued to bar the road against the advance of the crowd, had called upon them to disperse, and had opened fire on them in the event of their continued advance, his chances would have depended on the intimidating effect of two or three volleys, delivered at close quarters into the crowd massed along the highway and overflowing it on either side. If this produced a panic, the watchmen might have been used to complete the dispersal of the mob, and possibly to arrest its leaders; if the resolution of the crowd held firm, they must have borne down all opposition by sheer weight of numbers.

The matter was not put to the test. At this point there comes on the scene a somewhat ambiguous figure, that of Sardar Harcharan Singh, a local landholder. He was with the Sub-Inspector, and offered to go forward and parley with the crowd. He found them in a singular state of fierce excitement. Their leaders told him bluntly that the crowd had no intention of dispersing, that they were firmly resolved to advance to the police station, and thence over the railway crossing, through Chaura Bazaar and on to Mundera. Certain imputations of treachery and double-dealing were cast upon Harcharan Singh after the event, but he seems to have been honestly perturbed by what he had seen and heard. He was convinced that nothing could stop these men if once they resumed their forward march, and he believed himself to have obtained some sort of assurance from their leaders that, if they were not opposed, they would march past the police station, quietly and without disorder, on their way to Mundera. He suggested to the Sub-

Inspector that his men should be withdrawn within the station enclosure, adding that it would be easier "to deal with" the crowd after they had passed on. It is impossible to blame the ill-starred Sub-Inspector for accepting this advice. He withdrew his men accordingly, and the demonstrators resumed their forward march.

Gupteshar Singh had made a fatal mistake. Even if the Volunteers had had no other object in view than to impose their will on the recalcitrant shopkeepers of Mundera, the priceless advantage of the opportunity now offered them of keeping the Sub-Inspector and his men blockaded within the limits of the police station must have been apparent to their leaders. Apart, however, from this, they had their account to settle with Gupteshar Singh; they had come there "to ask the reason why" he had assaulted one or more of their number. Personally, I have not the slightest doubt that the phrases in which they had formulated their purpose implied something far beyond a mere desire for information; the spirit which inspired them was that of the Cornishmen who demanded to know "the reason why" King James II. was oppressing Bishop Trelawney. While, therefore, a section of the crowd pursued their march towards, and over, the railway crossing, a considerable body came to a halt in front of the open gateway of the police station and demanded to see the Sub-Inspector. The tone adopted by their leaders was insulting and provocative, but Gupteshar Singh adhered at first to the line of conduct he had marked out for himself and spoke them fair. It is obvious that he denied having beaten anyone except Bhagwan, for the explanation he offered was limited to the case of this man. He told the crowd that he did not recognise Bhagwan as a 'brother' of theirs; the man was a Government pensioner and might fairly be regarded as subject to the Sub-Inspector's authority. I doubt if his explanation went further than this, though statements were subsequently made attributing to him expressions of abject submission and apology. Whatever he said, his words were received, not merely with satisfaction, but with insolent and mocking triumph. A coarse jest ran through the crowd, attributing, with a Rabelaisian turn of phrase such as peasants love, certain consequences of abject terror to the Sub-Inspector personally, to the police generally, or to that abstract concept 'the Government.' Along with this came a derisive clapping of hands, such as had driven the interfering *brahman* from the meeting at Dumri.

For whatever errors of judgment Gupteshar Singh committed that day, he paid the ultimate price; his explanation was to be taken by no earthly tribunal. He had certainly been provoked to the limits of mortal endurance, but I can see no reason why his next step should be attributed to loss of temper. It is quite conceivable that the insolent triumph of his opponents served to bring home to his mind the true character of the position into which he had allowed himself to drift. His duty was to protect the shopkeepers of Mundera in the exercise of their lawful rights; the armed police had been placed at his disposal to enable him to discharge that duty efficiently. Was he to remain, cowering behind their muskets within the police station enclosure, while the National Volunteers taught the folk of Mundera that their will was the law of the land? Nor was this by any means the worst that could be anticipated. Suppose the baser elements of the crowd got out of hand, and the market was delivered over to plunder and arson, would not his superiors ask what he was doing the while? His first and most obvious duty was to recover his own freedom of action by clearing the space immediately in front of the station gateway. He may or he may not have attempted to comply with the letter of the law by issuing a formal order calling on the assembly to disperse; the evidence on the point was conflicting, and in the existing temper of the crowd it mattered little whether or not such a summons was issued. What is certain is that the Sub-Inspector refrained, even at this stage, from calling on the armed police: he sent forward his village watchmen, with orders to clear the strip of road in front of the police station. That they used some degree of force in the attempt is likely enough, though Sardar Harcharan Singh, who certainly saw what happened, and does not strike one as other than an impartial witness, deposed that they merely started the crowd on the run by thumping the ends of their staves on the ground, a reasonable method of attempting the dispersal of a largely barefoot crowd.

At the subsequent trial direct evidence was given that the Volunteers had been instructed that they were to attack the Sub-Inspector, if his answer to the question "why he had beaten our men" proved unsatisfactory; also, according to another witness, that the Volunteers were not to strike the first blow, "but if he" (the Sub-Inspector) "beat us we should beat him." This evidence came from a tainted source, and was hotly challenged on behalf of the defence, but the plain story of the events which immediately followed shows that the leaders of the demonstration had laid their plans beforehand for a collision between their followers and the police, to take place in the immediate neighbourhood of Chaura Police Station. As the throng in front of the entrance scattered before the advance of the watchmen, the cry went up that the police were beating the Volunteers. All up the line the whistles shrilled out the order to halt, and to turn back. That section of the crowd which had already passed over the railway crossing swung back, and there, stretching far away on either hand, lay the line of metals, with its ballast providing an inexhaustible supply of dangerous missiles. On this the crowd threw themselves; the improvised ammunition was passed on to those already in conflict with the police force near the station entrance. From two sides at once, north and east, the Sub-Inspector and his men found themselves assailed by an increasing shower of missiles. Now, if ever, the muskets of the armed police must be thrown into the scale, and the ill-starred Gupteshar Singh committed the final and fatal blunder of ordering the first volley to be fired in the air. Instantly the cry went up that 'Mahatmaji' was turning the bullets to water; "fiercer came the pelting," and the mob—a quite sufficient proportion of them by this time provided with weapons for hand-to-hand combat—charged home. When the doomed policemen began to fire in earnest, they shot two of their assailants dead, and inflicted perhaps a score of other casualties, mostly buck-shot wounds, whose trifling nature bore ample testimony to the inefficient loading of the cartridges used. Except that a majority of the village watchmen were allowed to slip away in the confusion, the victorious mob gave no quarter; it was by a mere accident that one constable survived. It may be doubted whether the armed police fired as much as two rounds apiece before they broke, losing all formation and concert, vainly seeking shelter inside the police station buildings, where they were butchered in detail. The police armoury was stormed and its store of weapons passed into the hands of the mob. Sub-Inspector Gupteshar Singh, twelve policemen, and ten village watchmen perished in the massacre. Fed by supplies of oil, looted from shops in the Chaura market, fire was employed to destroy the police buildings and to force out any policemen sheltering therein. When all was over attempts were made to dispose of the corpses by flinging them into the burning buildings; it is to be hoped, rather than concluded with any certainty, that no bodies were so treated in which life was not already extinct. All the official records of the police station were utterly destroyed. The captured *lathis* of the village watchmen were broken to fragments and police turbans torn into minute pieces. On one or more of the corpses left lying outside the ruined buildings shoes were laid, a gesture of ultimate insult and contempt.

If further evidence be needed to support the suggestion that something in the nature of a preconceived plan lay at the back of this appalling outbreak of savagery and mob violence, it is to be noted that it was found possible, as the attack on the police station developed, to detail sections of the mob for subsidiary operations. Numbers proceeded direct to the neighbouring railway station and post office, where they overcame the officials in charge and prevented telegrams from being sent to summon assistance from Gorakhpur. Moreover, the telegraph wires were cut, and a considerable breach effected in the railway line on the Gorakhpur side of Chaura Station.

When the work was done the crowd dispersed to their homes. I have seen photographs, taken on the following morning, of the scene they left behind them—the fire-scorched ruins of the police buildings, the corpses scattered on the trampled ground,—photographs so gruesome that they were never published, or even incorporated in any official record. Yet all the evidence shows that the mob departed in a spirit of exultation, openly boasting of their achievement, intoxicated with a short-lived sense of triumph and of power. There is grim irony in the cries raised by some of the departing groups, proclaiming that "the kingdom of Mahatmaji Gandhi was come."

CHAPTER II.

THE STORY OF THE TRIAL.

THE observer who studies India through Western eyes is apt to lose his bearings in a mirage of paradox; on the other hand, those with long experience of the country are inclined to settle down, too readily perhaps, to the conviction that things happen in India, quite in the ordinary course of events, which would be simply inconceivable as occurring in any other sort of environment. These remarks occurred to me as soon as I set myself to answer the self-propounded question: how would an ideally wise and just Government have dealt with this affair of the Chauri Chaura massacre?

From one point of view, undoubtedly, the peasants who stormed Chaura Police Station were simply rebels against the established Government. They set out on their march with cries of "Victory to Mahatmaji Gandhi"; they hailed their victory with acclamations, triumphantly proclaiming that they had established his 'kingdom.' 'Mahatma Gandhi' they unquestionably regarded as the embodiment of opposition to the Government under which they lived. Now to Western ideas the principles by which a wise and just Government will be guided in dealing with a revolt against its authority are obvious enough. First of all there must be prompt and effective measures to put down opposition, to teach the rebels the lesson of their own impotence. Next, the leaders and organisers of the rising must be sought out and sternly punished. Once this has been done the widest possible amnesty must be extended to their deluded followers, coupled with earnest investigation of the grievances, whether real or imaginary, which had roused them to action.

As applied to the facts under consideration, this programme breaks down at the very outset. There was no opposition to be put down, no lesson to be taught which the supposed pupils did not already know by heart. If this was an uprising against the established Government it came to an abrupt end after a single engagement, which had resulted in an overwhelming victory for the 'rebels.' Officials from Gorakhpur had reached Chauri Chaura Railway Station before midnight; not only was there no resistance to overcome, but within many miles of the ruined police station there was a wholesale absconding of 'National Volunteers' and others who knew themselves to be implicated, or thought themselves in danger of being implicated, in the affair. The sense of triumph, the sort of intoxication which follows on the shedding of blood in fierce encounter and the butchery of vanquished enemies, proved of brief duration. Before the next morning's sun rose the wretched peasants knew well enough that no new 'kingdom' had been set up; each man felt himself marked out for the vengeance of the irresistible power which, in a moment of madness, he had challenged. There was no rival authority to which they could appeal for countenance or support. It was given out that Mahatma Gandhi was overwhelmed with horror at the news of their exploit, and proposed to expiate by days of rigorous fasting the crime which had been committed by men who called upon his name. The organisers of the 'National Volunteers' cried out that they had only enrolled men whom they had bound down by solemn pledges to abstain from violence under all conceivable circumstances. The utmost they could do to help the terrified fugitives from justice was to suggest that this orgy of massacre on the part of men so pledged could only have resulted from some intolerable provocation offered by the police.

The affair was not to be appraised by Western standards; it eluded any attempt to handle it according to Western ideas or precedents. It was futile to treat this mob of deluded peasants as 'rebels,' and impolitic to dignify their riot by framing indictments for such high-sounding offences as "waging war on the king," or "conspiracy to deprive the King-Emperor of the sovereignty of British India." Still less was it possible to proclaim martial law in a district which, after one fierce blaze had burnt itself out, had subsided into a panic-stricken submission. The only alternative was to deal with the offenders as ordinary criminals, and to employ against them the cumbrous machinery of the ordinary law. They had committed offences enough against sections of the Indian Penal Code quite other than those dealing with crimes against the state. The gathering at Dumri could be treated as a 'criminal conspiracy,' on the mere ground that it was an attempt to coerce by concerted action shopkeepers of Mundera in the exercise of their legal rights, and to overawe by show of force the policemen detailed for their protection. At Chaura offences had been committed of rioting with murder, as well as arson and some looting of public and private property, to say nothing of wilful damage to the railway line and telegraph posts. The real difficulty lay in the collection of evidence sufficient to secure the conviction of individual rioters, the preparation of a list of the accused persons to be put on their trial and the working out of methods of procedure which should make it possible, within the limits of the ordinary law, to arrange for the satisfactory trial of a case in which the evidence promised to be voluminous and the number of accused persons unusually large.

In one respect the Government was fortunate; there was an officer of exceptional qualifications for the task ready to take the threads of the investigation into his own hands. Mr C. E. W. Sands was at that time Deputy Inspector-General of Police, in charge of a circle which included the Gorakhpur district. Speaking for myself, I never quite understood why Mr Sands was eventually permitted to retire from the service without that promotion to the Inspector-Generalship of the Province which must have come to him inevitably, if appointments in the Indian services always went to the ablest men available. Perhaps his action in this very case suggests a reason for his failure to reach the top of the tree. He was too ready to leave merely routine duties to look after themselves, when he conceived that an emergency had arisen which required him to devote all his energies to something not quite in the line of his ordinary work. Here was a case of altogether exceptional gravity and importance, in which the actual criminals numbered over three thousand men. Routine procedure required that the investigating police officer should draw up a complete list of those individuals against whom sufficient evidence of actual complicity in the affair was, in his opinion, available. All of these must either be proceeded against before a magistrate, with a view to their being committed for trial, or placed upon a list of absconded offenders in the event of their arrest not being effected. The Indian legislature has declined to place in police hands the power of saying: "There is evidence available sufficient to secure the conviction of such-an-one of having committed such-and-such an indictable offence, but the public interests do not require that he should be proceeded against." My own opinion, indeed, is that the provisions of the law in India regarding the powers and duties of the Public Prosecutor require further consideration; at anyrate something requires to be done before it can be said that we possess in all districts an adequate and reliable prosecuting agency.

In this particular case, the Government Advocate stated in the High Court that the police investigation had resulted in the discovery of evidence implicating at least one thousand persons; the number of accused persons finally placed on their trial was two hundred and twenty-five. A considerable amount of selection and discrimination obviously required to be exercised before the number could be reduced even to this extent. Over and above this, it was incumbent on the police officer in charge of the investigation to advise the Committing Magistrate in the matter of exercising the power, vested in him by law, of tendering a pardon to one or more of the accused persons with a view to securing his evidence, as an approver, against his fellow criminals. Two such witnesses were eventually produced at the trial.

In one other respect the investigation of this offence called for the most careful supervision.

The case concerned the massacre of twenty-three policemen of various ranks, who perished in the execution of their duty. Policemen are human beings. Those of them who were engaged in investigating this crime would have required to be something more or something less, if they were expected to contemplate with indifference the question of the punishment or escape of the offenders. On this point I am glad to quote from the judgment of the High Court :—

> " The close and unremitting supervision exercised by Mr C. E. W. Sands over the course of the investigation is apparent on almost every page of the record, and we are doing him no more than the barest justice in stating our opinion that it has been of incalculable service. The spirit in which the police investigation was conducted was in our opinion straightforward and worthy of commendation. Practically no suggestions to the contrary have been put forward. Had the police been so minded they could have caused weak evidence to be supplemented by persons who could have spoken to circumstances involving the accused and whose evidence would, from the position of the witness, have been invested with an air of truth. They could also, by similar oblique methods, have secured evidence of identification. We have detected nothing of this kind ; indeed, on the contrary there is a marked abstention from any wrong-doing of this sort."

Considering all the difficulties with which they had to contend, the police carried out their investigation with great promptitude. Proceedings in the court of the Committing Magistrate commenced on 25th March 1922, just seven weeks from the date of the crime. The Magistrate completed his proceedings by 18th June, and the trial at Sessions opened three days later. The recording of evidence continued steadily until 23rd October, and the last date on which any witness was examined was 30th October. Then the Sessions Judge had to settle down to the task of preparing his judgment. He had not merely to formulate his conclusions regarding the general course of events, but to sift out and appraise the evidence as it affected each individual accused.

His judgment was delivered on 9th January 1923. Three of the accused had died during the pendency of the trial, and as against one other the Public Prosecutor withdrew the case. This was done by reason of the man's state of health; I mention the fact to show that the power to enter a 'nolle prosequi' was actually exercised. There were forty-seven accused in respect of whom the Sessions Judge came to the conclusion that the charges were not proved: these he acquitted altogether, and there were two others whom he found guilty only of a minor offence. That left one hundred and seventy-two accused who were convicted upon a variety of charges, the gravest of which was that of murder committed in the course of a riot. For the benefit of English readers I ought, perhaps, to explain in greater detail the way in which a case of this sort is treated by the Indian Penal Code. One has to begin with the definition of a 'wrongful assembly,' a gathering of five or more persons for any one of various purposes which the law declares to be unlawful. If force or violence is used by any member of an 'unlawful assembly,' in pursuance of the 'common object' of the assembly, then each and every member of the same is guilty of 'rioting.' Finally, section 149 of the Code provides, in effect, that if any graver offence (*e.g.*, that of murder) is committed by one or more of the 'rioters,' in furtherance of their 'common object,' then each one of them is liable to punishment for that offence as if he had himself committed it. Considered with reference to the facts of this particular case, the provision is obviously just. Putting on one side, for the moment, all question as to what was in the minds of the organised crowd of demonstrators as they marched on Chaura Police Station, there can be no doubt that, from the moment the first volley was fired and the mob closed in on the doomed policemen, their object was to kill. Every individual who hurled a missile or joined in the rush was lending the weight of his co-operation towards that overwhelming mass which bore down all resistance. Morally as well as legally he shared the guilt of those who hunted down and battered the life out of their vanquished enemies. Granted the adequacy of the evidence in each case, the conviction of these hundred and seventy-two men on the charge of murder was right, and indeed inevitable. Now, by the law of England, when a man is found guilty of murder the only sentence which can be passed upon him is that of death; the question of the execution, commutation or remission of that sentence is left to the clemency of the Crown. In India the law allows the Judge an alternative; he may sentence either to death or to transportation for life. This limited power of discrimination is, however, hedged in with a very definite condition. The death sentence is recognised as ordinarily right and appropriate; if the Judge elects to pass the lesser sentence, he must give his reasons for so doing. In this case, the Sessions Judge gravely recorded his considered opinion that he was unable to formulate any valid reason why sentence of death should not be passed on each of the men whom he had found guilty. This being so, he followed the only course open to him when he sentenced one hundred and seventy-two men to death.

In England a Communist newspaper published the fact under the heading of "Indian Mass Murder," described it as an "act of Imperialist butchery," and suggested that it could only be averted by the "threat of direct action by the home proletariat." In India everyone knew that no capital sentence can be carried out until it has been confirmed by the High Court. There was some outcry, but on the whole a general recognition of the fact that the matter was still *sub judice*, and a tendency to refrain from comment until the High Court had spoken the final word. The Sessions Judge had taken infinite pains over the trial, and had written a most admirable judgment. In reviewing his proceedings the High Court dealt with this point in the following words :—

> "We do not, however, agree with the learned Sessions Judge that it is impossible to formulate such reasons" (*i.e.*, reasons why sentence of death should not be passed) "in respect of any of the appellants whose conviction on the capital charge we have affirmed. We do not think it expedient to say too much on this point, for we in no way desire to extenuate the savage nature of the crime or to come forward as apologists for the lawlessness of the crowd. We take account, nevertheless, of the fact that this crime grew out of a political agitation. The appellants are in the main ignorant peasants; the great majority of them were drawn into the business by misrepresentations of fact and preposterous promises concerning the millennium of *Swarāj*, the arrival of which was to be forwarded by courage and resolution on their part."

I am reluctant to add anything in this place, but I have one point to make. I would ask those interested in the welfare of India seriously to consider whether the system which makes every conviction in a case of any importance subject to an appeal on the facts, and every capital sentence subject to confirmation by a higher tribunal, does not involve the drawback, that it at least tends to weaken the sense of responsibility in the trial courts. I know the high sense of duty which always governed the conduct of the Judge who tried the Chauri Chaura case. If I could put the question to him, I am quite certain he would reply that he weighed and pondered the question of sentence with anxious thought and scrupulous care, and that his decision was governed by no consideration whatsoever beyond a desire to carry out the duty laid upon him by law. Assuming this to be his answer, I retain my doubt whether that incalculable factor, his subconscious mind, was not under the influence of the knowledge that ultimate responsibility for the judicial confirmation of the sentences passed by him lay elsewhere.

I have kept no note of the precise date on which the hearing of the appeals, duly presented by the hundred and seventy-two convicts, was commenced in the High Court. Our final decision was delivered on 30th April 1923, very nearly one and a quarter years after the commission of the offence. The case was admirably argued by a strong Bar, the Local Government having provided at the public expense counsel to represent those appellants who were too poor to engage anyone to speak for them. We had before us an exhaustive review of the evidence, both in respect of the general course of events and as affecting individual appellants, in the judgment of the Sessions Court. The voluminous evidence and a large number of exhibits had been translated and printed. Before the hearing closed, we had available type-written slips on which had been worked out, by the joint labour of counsel on both sides, a complete statement of the evidence against each individual appellant, supported by references to the pages of the printed record, and supplemented by a summary of his defence and of the evidence, if any, by which it was supported. The hearing in the High Court lasted fully four weeks, and our judgment covers ninety-six pages of print.

At the outset we had to deal with two arguments of a general nature. The first related to the possible prejudice involved, as regards each individual accused, in the fact that he was tried for his life along with two hundred and twenty-four other persons. Regarding this we could say little, except that the matter was one within the discretion of the trial court, and that everything humanly possible had been done to ensure that the evidence against each single accused should be fully weighed, and considered with as much attention as if he alone had been on his trial. In one respect, undoubtedly, this massing together of over two hundred accused in a single trial had hampered the prosecution rather than the defence. The reader will remember that Sub-Inspector Gupteshar Singh had collected about him a body of forty or more village watchmen, of whom at least thirty escaped from the final massacre. Several of these gave important evidence bearing on the identification of particular accused. They were illiterate peasants, often belonging to one of the menial castes. Here and there individuals amongst them had recognised in the raging mob that closed in upon the police station one or more faces of men previously known to them, but to a considerable extent their evidence related to the identification of some individual, previously unknown to the witness, whom he recognised after arrest and had picked out at some 'identification parade.' Let the intelligent reader exercise his imagination to put himself in the place of one of these witnesses, appearing before the Sessions Judge to give his evidence, some time in July or August, five or six months after the events to which he is deposing. Rising tier above tier, arranged along the wooden benches specially constructed for the purposes of the trial, stand the serried ranks of the accused. Some time last April or May the witness has pointed out to the Committing Magistrate, perhaps one, perhaps two or three, of these men as individuals whose face or figure had impressed itself on his memory, when he saw the man taking such-and-such a part in the assault on the police station or the final massacre. He is now called upon to repeat the identification. Is it to be wondered at that mistakes were made which discounted the value of some of the testimony on which the prosecution relied? On the other hand, of course, the circumstances served to give one confidence in the value of certain identifications, unhesitatingly made, first at some parade of suspected persons and others in the presence of a responsible officer, then before the Committing Magistrate, and again at the Sessions Trial.

The second point taken related to the alleged "misjoinder of charges." It challenged more particularly the propriety of including in one and the same trial charges relating to what was done, or agreed to be done, in the course of the gathering at Dumri, and others in respect of the crimes of murder, arson, and robbery committed, perhaps a couple of hours later, at Chaura Police Station. The point is a highly technical one, and it would require a regular treatise to make it intelligible, in all its bearings, to the lay reader. Lawyers will understand me readily enough when I say that the question is, to my mind, essentially one of the relevancy of evidence. The mischief of trying a man at one trial in respect of two unconnected charges is that he may be prejudiced in respect of each one of them by evidence legally admissible in respect of the other only. No such difficulty could arise in the present case. It being alleged against the accused *A.* that he took part in the commission of certain murders at Chaura Police Station, at or about a certain hour on 4th February 1922, evidence would be admissible to prove that *A.* had been seen a couple of hours earlier at a place two miles distant from Chaura, in the company of other persons proved to have been concerned in the murders, and that he there entered into an agreement with them that they should march together to the said police station. My own opinion is that the somewhat complicated provisions of the Indian Criminal Procedure Code on the subject of the joinder of charges might usefully be simplified by the enactment that any number and description of charges might be tried together, subject to the proviso that no evidence should be offered in respect of any one charge which would not be legally admissible in respect of each and all of them.

On the broad facts of the case, as apart from the complicity of particular individuals, there was not very much to be said on behalf of the appellants. It was strenuously contended that the assembly at Dumri, and the resolutions there taken, did not involve an agreement to do any criminal act. We were asked to hold, in effect, that the entire body of close on two thousand National Volunteers marched to Chaura simply in order to put to Sub-Inspector Gupteshar Singh certain questions which they had a perfect right to ask; further, that the demonstration contemplated at Mundera amounted to nothing more than what might be called the 'peaceful picketing' of certain obnoxious shops. From these premises the conclusion was deduced that the police had made an unprovoked and illegal attack upon men who were peacefully passing along the front of Chaura Police Station, in the discharge of their duty as law-abiding citizens. The question whether the said citizens would, even upon this view of the case, have been justified in slaughtering the Sub-Inspector and twenty-two of the men under his orders was not, and could not, be seriously raised.

The facts established by the evidence I have already set forth in the story of the riot. The most sinister question arising out of that story was never completely answered. Was the murder of Sub-Inspector Gupteshar Singh, and incidentally of any policeman who might seek to protect him, present to the minds of the organisers of the assembly at the Dumri threshing-floor as the ultimate goal of the enterprise they had in hand, or at least as an event extremely likely to be brought about by the prosecution of that enterprise? The reader must draw his own conclusions from the facts which I have laid before him. The judgment of the High Court concluded the paragraph dealing with the appropriate punishment of the offenders with the following words:—

> "We cannot take leave of this case without an uneasy feeling that there are individuals at large at this moment, men who have not even been put on their trial in connection with this affair, whose moral responsibility for what took place at Chaura police station on the afternoon of 4th February 1922, is at least equal to that which rests upon such men as Nazar Ali and Lal Mohammed, who acted as leaders openly in the light of day, and at least placed their own lives on the hazard along with the rest."

Turning to the fate of the hundred and seventy-two men sentenced to death at the Gorakhpur Sessions, it may be summarised as follows:—

Died in prison, pending the hearing of their appeals	2
Acquitted by the High Court	38
Sentence of death confirmed by the High Court .	19
Conviction affirmed, but sentence reduced to transportation for life	110
Convicted on the lesser charge of simple rioting .	3
Total	172

The great majority of the acquittals turned on a question of principle. The Sessions Judge had convicted no one on the murder charge who was not directly implicated in the evidence given by one or both of the approvers. He had accepted the principle, ordinarily insisted upon by all the courts in India, that a man shall not be found guilty of any offence on the testimony of an accomplice, unless that testimony is in some way corroborated, not merely in general, but as regards the complicity of the individual whose case is under consideration. He had, however, held that the fact that a particular accused person was an enrolled Volunteer was, under the circumstances of this case, sufficient corroboration, as against him, of the accomplice evidence. The High Court refused to accept this principle, largely on the ground that the crime had not been the work of the National Volunteers alone, and that it could be proved by figures that there must have been somewhere about a thousand enrolled Volunteers, residing within marching distance of Chaura Police Station, who had not joined in the demonstration.

The Chief Justice and I had not completed our task even when an anxious scrutiny of the evidence affecting each individual appellant had brought us to the results already set forth. We had to consider whether we were prepared to recommend any, and if so which, of the one hundred and ten appellants, in respect of whom we could pass no lesser sentence than that of transportation for life, to the Local Government as fit subjects for the clemency of the Crown. In India, moreover, it is customary for the Judges, when making such a recommendation, to indicate the exact punishment which would in their opinion suffice to meet the justice of the case. A further review of the facts proved against each of these men was therefore necessary, together with the consideration of any circumstances, such as the age or infirmity of the offender, which might reasonably affect the question of punishment.

In the result, we submitted no recommendation in respect of fourteen men who were left to undergo the sentence of transportation for life. The measure of their guilt fell, in our opinion, only just below that of the ringleaders and actual murderers in respect of whom we had confirmed the sentence of death.

The remainder we classified as follows :—

Recommended to undergo rigorous imprisonment for		
	eight years	19 men
,, ,,	five years	57 men
,, ,,	three years	20 men

Our recommendations were given immediate and precise effect to by the Local Government.

The actual result of the prolonged trial, therefore, was that nineteen of the rioters were hanged, fourteen were transported for life, and nineteen others received a really severe sentence of imprisonment. I may be permitted in conclusion to raise two questions.

The first is whether, on the whole, the interests

of justice would not have been better served if only these fifty-two men had been placed on their trial, and all else covered up by a proclamation of amnesty issued as soon as possible after the conclusion of the proceedings in the court of the Committing Magistrate.

The second is whether it is too much to expect that a result, at least approximating to the above, might have been brought about if, after the conclusion of the proceedings in the Magistrate's Court, a short interval had been allowed for a careful review of the case and scrutiny of the entire evidence on the part of a Public Prosecutor possessing, and meriting, the entire confidence of the Government.

I am quite aware that more than one answer is possible to each of these questions. I can only state what I should myself have done if I had been the Sessions Judge who received the Magistrate's order committing two hundred and twenty-five persons for trial before me on a capital charge. I should have recorded some such order as the following :—

"The law allows me to try these men either jointly or separately ; the matter is within my discretion. By reason, possibly, of some defect of intellect or training, I do not consider myself capable of trying such a number of men, or anything approximating to such a number, at one single trial so as to do justice to the case of each one of them. I propose, therefore, to try these men in three batches. Allowing the Public Prosecutor reasonable time in which to consider his position, I suggest that he should furnish me with a list of the seventy-five accused against whom he has the strongest evidence, or whose conviction he considers most desirable in the interests of justice. Failing this, I shall be compelled, reluctantly, to begin with the first seventy-five men in alphabetical order."

Now, the triplication of the trial would, of course, have been practically impossible. The inconvenience inflicted on the unhappy witnesses, and the strain on everyone concerned, would make the thing unthinkable. My procedure would, therefore, have led to one of two results. Quite possibly, I should have been hastily transferred from Gorakhpur and replaced by a Judge who had greater confidence in his own abilities. On the other hand, it is conceivable that the Public Prosecutor would have reconsidered his position and produced a list of seventy-five men, or thereabouts, whose trial was really necessary. In respect of the remainder it would have been competent for him to enter a *nolle prosequi*, and I should have felt that I had " done the State some service."

VII.

MISUNDERSTANDINGS.

What I may call the classical story about a conversation at cross-purposes between an Englishman and an Indian is something of a chestnut, but I have met with Anglo-Indians who did not seem to have heard it before. It deserves such immortality as I can give it. A sergeant has got into trouble for assaulting his table servant. His defence before the Cantonment Magistrate is as follows :—

" Yes, I know it's wrong to hammer these fellows, and I don't do it. You can ask the man if I ever laid a finger on him before. But there is a limit to all things. This was at breakfast, and they served me up a ' muttony-chap,' as they call it, that I couldn't get a knife into, let alone my teeth. This fellow Abdul here was standing just behind my chair. I looks round at him, and I says—

" ' This meat's beastly tough ' ; that was all I did say.

" ' Yes, Sahib,' says he, ' suck it ' !

" Well—I couldn't be expected to stand that, could I ? "

Now, there is a Hindustani word which may be phonetically transliterated as *suck-utt,* and it means 'hard' or 'tough'; the faithful Abdul was merely expressing polite concurrence in his master's verdict on the breakfast joint.

There are occasions, however, when a fair degree of knowledge of the vernacular may only serve to create serious misunderstanding, as it did in a certain case which once came before me as Joint Magistrate at Budaun. I do not know if Thomas Atkins in India is still as fond of a day's miscellaneous shooting as he was thirty to forty years ago; probably his opportunities are much restricted nowadays. He used to pursue his sport on lines of his own, and with a recklessness as regards the range of a bullet fired from a military rifle which at times involved him in serious trouble. It seemed at first sight as if something of the sort must have happened in the case which I was called upon to investigate. A corporal and two privates from a regiment stationed at Bareilly had gone out by train for a little shooting in my district. On their return the corporal reported that they had been waylaid in the neighbourhood of a certain village by a party of men who had accused them, quite falsely, of having shot one of the villagers. The Cantonment authorities were naturally nervous on the point and asked for an investigation. It seemed odd that no report of such an occurrence had reached the district authorities; but inquiries were set on foot, and resulted in the appearance in my court of half a dozen residents of a village near the Bareilly border, charged with riotous conduct which had come near to provoking a disastrous breach of the peace.

The witnesses against them were the corporal and his two companions. They told their story with the most obvious good faith, and if they were speaking the truth, the conduct of the villagers had been outrageous to a degree. The three soldiers, moving through the scrub jungle in skirmishing order, had put up a fine boar. The animal showed considerable annoyance at being disturbed, and was in fact shot down in the act of charging. The delighted sportsmen contrived to sling the corpse on to one of their rifles for convenience of carriage, and started back for the wayside railway station at which they had alighted. Presently they were overtaken by a group of angry villagers who shouted to them to stop. The Corporal was the only one of the party who knew anything of the vernacular, and he was quite positive that what the villagers said as they came up was—

"Put down that pig; you have shot a man of ours!"

As it happened, only two shots had been fired by the party, and the two bullets were safe inside the body of the old boar. The corporal proceeded to explain the fact in such Hindustani as he could command, but the more he pointed to the two bullet wounds, the angrier the villagers seemed to grow, the more insistent on the claim they were obviously making that the pig should be handed over to them. As often as the corporal demanded to know the reason for their claim, he could get nothing out of them but repetitions of the phrase which had startled him in the first instance—"You have shot a man of ours!" He demanded to be shown the man they were alleged to have killed, and understood them to say that the man had been carried to his village, two or three miles away. He was not dead, but had apparently been wounded somewhere in the upper part of the leg. The villagers were angry that their assertions to this effect were not accepted without their being asked to produce the injured man.

Tempers were in fact getting frayed on both sides, and presently the group of peasants challenged the three Englishmen to fight.

"There are three of you," they said, "and ten of us; but you have your guns, and we have only our bamboos and a couple of axes. That makes it a fair fight. We are *thakurs* and always fight fairly; you are soldiers, and if you want to carry away the pig you should be prepared to fight for it."

Luckily the corporal kept his head; whatever happened he was not going to accept this challenge. Even if he and his companions were not killed on the spot, there would only be their word for it afterwards that they had fired in self-defence. He ostentatiously unloaded his rifle and laid it on the ground, ordering the other two to do the same.

"Our rifles are the property of Government," he said to the excited villagers; "we are forbidden to use them in a private quarrel. If you insist on carrying off the pig, you must take it, but it is robbery. The pig is ours; we killed it."

The *thakurs* were apparently taken aback. There was some discussion amongst them which the corporal could not follow, but finally their spokesman suggested a division of the animal. The suggestion worked like a charm. When the details came to be discussed it was found that those parts of the carcass which the Indians particularly wanted were precisely those for which the Englishmen had no use whatever. Knives were produced; the body was dismembered on the spot. Each party collected its allotted share and they parted quite good friends. I could see, indeed, that the accused *thakurs* felt honestly aggrieved that their late opponents had acted so meanly as to make a court case out of a dispute which had been thus amicably settled.

I pointed this out to the officer from Bareilly who had attended to conduct the prosecution on behalf of the Cantonment authorities. He replied, reasonably enough from his point of view, that Corporal Rogers was bound to obey a regulation requiring soldiers who had been allowed shooting permits to report any case of friction between themselves and villagers. Further, the conduct of the *thakurs* had been highly provocative; what right had they to demand even a share in the pig? And what did they mean by their assertion, apparently a pure falsehood invented to overawe the soldiers, that the latter had shot one of their fellows? There might have been very serious trouble indeed, if Corporal Rogers had not kept his head, and it was lucky that he had known enough of the vernacular to discuss the matter with the villagers. "As a matter of fact," he concluded, "we make it a rule not to allow the men to go out shooting unless at least one of the party can speak the language; but if this sort of thing is allowed to go unpunished we shall have to put the Budaun District out of bounds altogether."

I was already beginning to wonder whether the real cause of the trouble might not be that the worthy corporal knew a little too much of the language, or not quite enough. When I turned to the accused for their version of the quarrel, this soon became obvious. There is a word in the Hindustani language the essential meaning of which is 'to beat' or 'to strike'; it will be used by a villager where an Englishman would say 'to wound.' Moreover, it quite often means 'to kill,' pure and simple, and this is the sense in which it would be most familiar to an English soldier. Corporal Rogers was positive that the first definite phrase which had reached his ears, amidst the confused shouts of the pursuing villagers, was—

"Put down that pig: you have shot one of our men!"

What the villagers were saying was—

"Put down that pig: it has wounded one of our men."

The fact is, the *thakurs* were also sportsmen in their own way, and they had marked down that old boar; he had been doing more damage of late among their crops than they were prepared to stand. That very afternoon they had beaten him up out of his lair and driven him cunningly into the snare prepared for him, a line of nets fastened to stout posts. As they closed in to finish him off with bamboo quarterstaffs and axes, the powerful brute had torn through the meshes of the net. One of his assailants had gone down with a nasty gash above the knee, and the boar had broken away into the jungle. They may or may not have given him something to remember them by, but he was certainly not crippled in any way when the three soldiers blundered upon him, sullenly nursing his wrath in some thicket. The sound of their shots reached the *thakurs*, who had just arranged to have the wounded man carried to his house and were discussing the question whether the chase was worth following any further. Setting out in that direction, probably with no more definite purpose than that of finding out what had happened, they had overtaken the soldiers carrying off the kill. If they could prove that they had disabled, or seriously wounded the beast before the Englishmen shot him, they reckoned on the latter being sportsmen enough to admit that they had a prior claim to the trophy. The point could only be settled by an examination of the carcass, and this was all they intended to demand when they shouted "put down that pig." The fact that one of their fellows had been rather badly hurt in their recent encounter with the animal bulked so largely in their minds that the words "he has wounded a man of ours" seemed to them a mere summary of the story they had to tell by way of explaining their demand. What they actually said was: "has hit a man of ours," leaving the nominative to be understood. From their point of view, what could the nominative be, except 'the pig' aforementioned? It is at least arguable whether the simple villagers, if they had intended to say, "You have hit one of our men," would have used any different form of words; at anyrate there was nothing surprising in the fact that Corporal Rogers should have so interpreted them. His mind was preoccupied with admonitions as to the danger of rash or random shooting, and jumped to the conclusion that he and his men were being accused of having done the very thing they had been particularly warned against.

The discussion started on the basis of this misunderstanding could only grow more and more confused. Any attempt on the part of the villagers to explain that they claimed to have wounded the old boar before the soldiers shot him impinged vainly on the notion, now firmly fixed in the corporal's mind, that they were still talking about a man alleged to have been shot. On the other hand, his repeated requests to be shown the wounded man seemed to the *thakurs* mere attempts to evade the point really in dispute, besides being gratuitous aspersions on their veracity. When he pointed to the bullet wounds on the carcass, they thought he was insisting, quite superfluously, on the fact that it was the soldiers who had finished the animal off. That the affair ended without bloodshed was due, under Providence, to the tact and self-control of the corporal; the *thakurs* themselves admitted, when the whole thing had been explained to them, that they had been in the wrong. I could not pass over the matter without convicting them at least of the offence of 'wrongful assembly,' but they accepted with a good grace the light sentences I felt compelled to pass.

If one may venture on a generalisation, the Indian mind is nimbler and more subtle than the English; the one may fail to apprehend the other, even when the vehicle of speech is the same and there is no misunderstanding of the words used. I can illustrate this point by a story which I prefer to tell under a veil of anonymity. I was fortunate enough to be brought, at one stage of my career, into fairly close association with a Hindu gentleman of the highest class, whom I have always regarded as one of the greatest Indians of his time. A very learned lawyer, with an unequalled command of all the arts of advocacy, he was also a man of singularly clear judgment and unlimited public spirit. Over and above all this, the Pandit, as I am content to call him, won the esteem of all and the affection of many by an extraordinary grace of manner, a fine flower of courtesy deeply rooted in his essential goodness of heart. Amongst the many services he rendered his country was his membership of the Legislative Council of his Province. It so happened that in the said Council there was a very close division on a question which excited much party feeling and racial animosity. The Pandit, though present throughout the debate, abstained from voting. Not long afterwards a very exalted personage, in the course of a private interview, asked him point blank his reasons for so abstaining. His reply was a curious one; he threw the blame on the notoriously defective acoustics of the Council Chamber in which the matter had been debated. He had done his very best, he gravely asserted, to follow the arguments on both sides; finding the greater part of them absolutely inaudible, he had thought it right to reserve judgment. The answer produced an unfavourable impression upon his interlocutor. What, he asked indignantly, were you to think of a man who was not merely unable to make up his mind on a matter of great public importance, but who gave you such a reason as that for his inability? Now, to make up your mind to remain neutral in a matter upon which all those about you are vehemently taking sides, may require greater strength of character and a saner judgment than that of any of the disputants.

And as regards the form of the answer, I take leave to ask in my turn, whether the dear old gentleman could conceivably have intimated, with a more perfect urbanity and a daintier spice of humour, that he had been asked a question which he was perfectly entitled not to answer, and that he intended to stand upon that right.